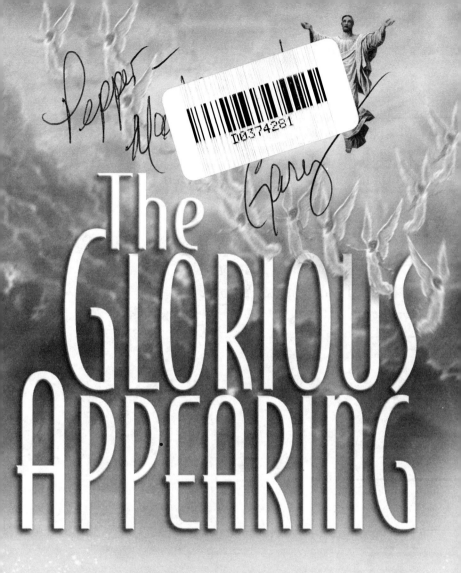

The GLORIOUS APPEARING

This book may prove to be
one of the most disturbing books
you will ever read,
but it will also be one
of the most critical.

Dedication

I want to dedicate this work to four men who shaped my life and encouraged me in my walk with my Lord Jesus Christ. I often pray for and thank my Savior for their influence upon me.

Laprell Frazier, my Dad
Reverend Dickson Rial, Pastor
Dr. H.D. McCarty, Pastor
Dr. J. Frank Davis, Pastor

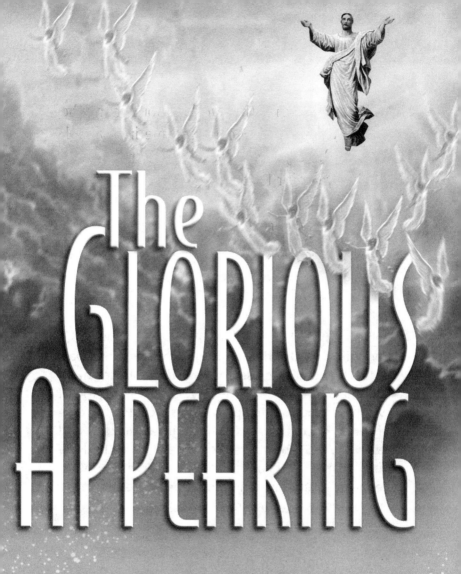

The GLORIOUS APPEARING

GARY FRAZIER

21st Century Press
P.O. Box 8033
Springfield, MO 65801

The Glorious Appearing

Copyright 2001, Gary Frazier

Discovery Ministries
Attention: Gary Frazier
P.O. Box 13770
Arlington, TX 76094

ISBN: 0-9700639-7-0

Cover Design: Lee Fredrickson: IBIS Design
Book Design: Lee Fredrickson: IBIS Design

Contents

Foreword

As we enter a new millennium there seems to be a renewed interest in the biblical prophecies and teachings surrounding the end times. The theme is prevalent in books, both Christian and secular, as well as in popular movies. To read or watch some of these works is to receive a potpourri of intrigue, mystery, make-believe and the latest in special effects, with only a smattering of biblical truth.

It is in this climate that I welcome my good friend Gary Frazier's book, *The Glorious Appearing*. Using the story of a typical American family as a backdrop, Dr. Frazier walks us through the sequence of events that is in the future for the believer and the non-believer. Through the eyes and experiences of the imaginary Rhodes family, we see the reality of death, eternity spent in Heaven or in Hell, the Rapture of the Church, the Judgment Seat of Christ or the Bema, the Marriage Supper, the Tribulation, the Second Coming, Armageddon, the Millennial Reign of Christ and the Great White Throne Judgment. For some of you these are familiar terms, while for others, well, you may think I'm speaking a foreign language! These are all specific events and periods of time that indeed will occur in the future. When these events will occur is known only to God. The specific dates will unfold according to His divine timetable. It is this timetable that Gary explains in great detail, defining the terminology and presenting the various theories or schools of thought surrounding the last days, as he is uniquely qualified to do. In recent years, Gary Frazier has virtually lived in the Holy Land, teaching, preaching, studying and observing, first hand, the current issues and happenings in the Middle East, and how they relate to the biblical prophecies surrounding that land. He has a great love and passion for Israel and its people, and an unquenchable interest in events, past, present and future surrounding its history. Because of this, I believe he has tremendous credibility as a teacher of biblical eschatology.

Although *The Glorious Appearing* is a theological study, it is illustrative and practical so that you do not have to be a theologian to understand it. Not only will you benefit from Gary's insight and instruction, you will experience his passion and sense of urgency for men and women to know God's plan for their lives and to receive His sacrificial offering of His only begotten Son.

If, after reading the chapters on Hell and the Tribulation, there is not a rekindling of an evangelistic passion in your heart, then something's wrong with you! Just imagine a world without the Church and Christ! That's what will happen at the appointed time in history. The horror and loneliness in Hell, and a world shaking its fist in the face of Almighty God, are depicted vividly in the contemporary account of the Rhodes. I believe this book will become not only a valuable instruction book and teaching aid, but also an effective evangelistic tool.

Death — it's real — it's final — and like the Rhodes family, it will happen to you and to me one day. Hebrews 9:27 tells us that, *it is appointed unto men once to die, but after this the judgment.* We all have a divine appointment, one we will keep, whether we want to or not. The reality of death is always with us, and with that reality comes the realization that we will face Almighty God. The bottom line of this meeting with our Creator will be what we have done with Jesus Christ.

So continue reading, and when you do, you will discover gold in these pages as you are compelled to examine your own heart and life and are drawn to Jesus Christ — the One who will come again to rule and reign throughout eternity, and before whom every knee will bow and every tongue will confess "King of kings and Lord of lords."

—Ed Young, Senior Pastor
Second Baptist Church, Houston, Texas

 Charles Dickens' immortal novel *Tale of Two Cities* begins with the unforget-table line, "It was the best of times; it was the worst of times." That same senti-ment could well explain the experience awaiting two groups of people in the end time. For those who know Jesus Christ as personal Savior, the end will be the best of times. For those who do not know Him, the end will be the worst of times.

While we live in a seemingly diverse world, there are really only two kinds of people — two kinds of people with two kinds of destinies. For those who know the Lord Jesus Christ, there will a destiny of resurrection if one has died and immedi-ate translation into the air with the Lord if one is alive when Jesus returns. For those who do not know the Lord, there will be a destiny of conscious torment for the dead and a hell on earth for those left behind after Christians are caught away.

How do we know this? The Bible! The Bible does not leave us ignorant of those things ahead. While it does not give every detail about the future and the life beyond, the Bible most definitely does give us all the "need to know" information to prepare us for the last days.

In the chapters ahead we will explore the destiny of those who know the Lord Jesus Christ as personal Savior and those who have rejected Him as Lord of life. We will follow a time line, a chronology, of the events to come. Along that time line, we will show what will happen to both the believer and the unbeliever. There will be starkly contrasting destinies for the two.

In this context, you will be introduced to two generations of the Rhodes family of Normal, Ohio. Harold Rhodes died in 1960 and went straight to hell. His wife Betty followed him in death four years later. She loved the Lord Jesus Christ and immediately went to be with Him in heaven. You will follow the destinies of these two senior Rhodes. Then you will meet Harold and Betty's son Henry, who is left behind at the Rapture of the Church and also lives through the unprecedented trials of the Tribulation. At the same time, you will follow the destiny of Henry's wife Helen, a devout believer who experiences the Rapture, the Judgment Seat of Christ, the Marriage Supper of the Lamb, the Second Coming of Jesus, the Thousand-Year Reign of Christ and the Eternal Order.

The next event on God's timetable will be the

Rapture or the coming of Christ for the saints, the saved. It is true that the word "rapture" does not occur in the biblical text itself. The word derives from the Latin *raptere* which means "to snatch away, to catch away." The word, however, is an excellent word to capture the meaning of St. Paul's description of the great scene in which living believers will be *"caught up"* to be with the Lord (1 Thessalonians 4:17). Those alive at that climactic moment will not, however, precede those believers who have died before that time. They shall be raised from the dead and lead the vanguard into the heavens above. Those living believers shall follow immediately behind them.

On the other hand, those who are not believers will be left behind. The Lord Jesus makes this very clear. He indicated this stark truth in the words, *Then two men will be in the field: one will be taken and the other left. Two women will be grinding at the mill: one will be taken and the other left* (Matthew 24:40-41). The world as we know it will not end with the Rapture of the believers. There will be a great population left behind on planet earth. The Church will be gone, the Holy Spirit will be gone and the presence of Christ amidst His people will be gone. The world will get exactly what it always wanted — the total absence of Jesus Christ and His people.

Thus, after the Rapture there will begin a seven-year period Jeremiah the prophet referred to as *the time of Jacob's trouble* (Jeremiah 30:7). Jesus described it by saying, *For then there will be great tribulation, such as was not since the beginning of the world to this time, no, nor ever shall be* (Matthew 24:21). This unprecedented period will last for seven years (Daniel 9:27). Revelation 6:1-17 describes in detail the unleashing of horrible, unspeakable, unimaginable wrath on the God-forsaken planet. The world that rejected Christ will have the opportunity to live in a world without Him. Never in the imagination of depraved humanity could there be conceived what will happen during that time.

In the very midst of this period will be the desecration of the rebuilt temple (Matthew 24:15). The abomination of desolation will transpire (Daniel 9:27; 2 Thessalonians 2:2-4). The lost on earth will experience the full blast of these events.

But what of the saved in heaven? These seven years shall be a time of judgment of the saints based on the *quality* of their doctrine and life (1 Corinthians 3:11-17). This is the judgment of the *Bema* or the Judgment Seat of Christ. This will not be judgment for salvation or damnation. It will be a judgment of the quality of Christian life and doctrine. The result of the scrutiny will be the granting or the loss of rewards to believers on the basis of that quality. While all hell is breaking loose in the tribulation on earth below, the risen Christian will receive the appropriate reward in heaven.

At the end of that period will be the Second Coming of Christ, the coming of Christ with the saints (Matthew 24:29-31; Revelation 19:11-21). This will not be the sudden, silent, selective removal of the Church. This will be the glorious, visible return of the risen and reigning Christ. After the Battle of Armageddon, the victorious Christ will reign on earth for one thousand years (Revelation 20:1-6). The unbelievers who are alive at the return of Christ will live out their lives, die and go to hell awaiting their final judgment. The tribulation saints, those who are saved during the tribulation and are martyred, will immediately be transformed and join the returning army of Christ. At the end of the Thousand-Year Reign of Christ on the earth, there will be the final judgment of the lost. This will be a day of unimaginable despair in which the doomed and damned will be given their final sentence — endless torment in hell, forever separated from God and their loved ones. In the eternal state the saved will spend eternity with God in heaven and the lost will spend eternity with Satan and his demons in the fire of hell. What a division of humanity this shall be!

Matthew 24:1-14

And Jesus went out, and departed from the temple: and his disciples came to him for to shew him the buildings of the temple. And Jesus said unto them, See ye not all these things? verily I say unto you, There shall not be left here one stone upon another, that shall not be thrown down. And as he sat upon the Mount of Olives, the disciples came unto him privately, saying, Tell us, when shall these things be? and what shall be the sign of thy coming, and of the end of the world?

And Jesus answered and said unto them, Take heed that no man deceive you. For many shall come in my name, saying, I am Christ; and shall deceive many. And ye shall hear of wars and rumours of wars: see that ye be not troubled: for all these things must come to pass, but the end is not yet. For nation shall rise against nation, and kingdom against kingdom: and there shall be famines, and pestilences, and earthquakes, in divers places. All these are the beginning of sorrows. Then shall they deliver you up to be afflicted, and shall kill you: and ye shall be hated of all nations for my name's sake. And then shall many be offended, and shall betray one another, and shall hate one another. And many false prophets shall rise, and shall deceive many. And because iniquity shall abound, the love of many shall wax cold. But he that shall endure unto the end, the same shall be saved. And this gospel of the kingdom shall be preached in all the world for a witness unto all nations; and then shall the end come.

Chapter
One

The Reality of Mortality

As Queen Elizabeth lay dying, surrounded by the splendor of her palace, she uttered the famous words, "My kingdom for an inch of time." The most powerful woman in the world could not stop the falling shadow of death. George Burns was already booked to perform in Las Vegas on his 100th birthday, but he could not stop an earlier appointment with mortality. Young and handsome John F. Kennedy, Jr., and his beautiful wife had the same date. Revered football legend Tom Landry, who seemed to be immortal, could not stop the moment. The same day he died the beloved cartoonist of Peanuts fame, Charles Schultz, also died. None could stop the reality of mortality.

Our youth- and fitness-obsessed culture remains intoxicated with the allure of life that will not end. Even though there are more centenarians alive today than ever before, they too face mortality.

We are temporary. We are transient. Every grave marker in every cemetery on this planet is a witness to that reality. Go to the cemetery. Look at a granite marker. Visualize that inescapable fact that someday your name will be on a stone just like that, with a date of birth and a date of death. Unless you live in the generation that witnesses the Rapture of the Church, you will leave this planet by the same route as everyone else with the exception of Enoch and Elijah. Enoch walked with God and was not, that is, he was raptured away into heaven without ever having faced physical death. Elijah was caught up in a fiery chariot and likewise skipped death. I have never known anyone who had that experience, have you?

Unaccountably, the end of the twentieth century witnessed a fatal attraction to a famous shipwreck at the beginning of the century, the sinking of the *Titanic.* The world riveted its attention on the loss of a ship with more than 1,500 fatalities in the icy waters of the Atlantic. One young person in a tee-shirt at O'Hare airport in Chicago caught the truth of the matter. The tee-shirt read, "The ship sank; get over it." As a matter of fact, we are all on the *Titanic.* It is called planet earth. Nobody journeys forever.

One of the early psychiatrists mused that no

man can really contemplate his own death. That may indeed be the case. In our Internet, cell phone, fax machine, voice mail, overnight delivery, fast-track society, death seems to be an unpleasant interruption in the action. Yet no new technology has changed the old reality. Everybody dies. You have a date with death. No technology will change that. Some place their hope in cloning to preserve themselves forever. Others believe in cryogenics and have their mortal remains frozen until the day a cure will be found for their cause of death. Some actually believe that brains will be transplanted in the skulls of volunteers who will take on the old brain of a very rich person.

John D. Rockefeller, Sr., built the greatest fortune in American history until that of Bill Gates. He was the founder and power behind Standard Oil. He and his son spent the rest of their lives trying to give away all of the money that Rockefeller had made. As the richest man on the planet, Rockefeller had a single obsession: He wanted to stay alive. He founded hospitals and advanced research centers for the study of longevity. He meticulously studied the latest research on long life. He wanted to live to be a hundred. He died just short of that mark. The richest man in the world, with all of the resources to stave off the inevitable, could not stop it.

Every biography ends with an obituary. The pianist plays his last note. The carpenter hammers his final nail. The barber cuts his final head of hair. The homemaker washes her last dish. The athlete runs his final mile. The teacher utters her final lesson. Yet this generation, in a way unlike any other, lives with a blissful refusal to acknowledge this absolute reality. We are mortal.

I write these words to inform you of your mortality. You will die. But that will not be the end of you. Plants die and decompose. Animals die and their lives are gone forever. Human beings die and face another dimension of eternal existence. Ever since God breathed into Adam's nostrils the breath of life, every human that ever drew a breath on this planet lasts forever. Abraham and Sarah, Isaac and Rebekah, Pharaoh and Nebuchadnezzar, John the Baptist and Nero and the entire roll-call of humanity both famous and obscure will have a conscious existence forever.

So will you.

This book presents to you the two destinations that define the eternal existence of every individual who ever died. One destination holds inescapable horror and eternal retribution. The other is one of release, reward, rest and reunion. There could not be a greater contrast between the two.

Harold Rhodes died and went to hell. His wife Betty died and went to heaven. Their son Henry, an unbeliever like his father, lived through the Rapture, the Tribulation, entered the Millennial Reign, then died and later was resurrected to stand before the Great White Throne Judgment, sentenced, like his reprobate father, to an eternity in hell. In heaven, Betty gathered around the throne of God with her daughter-in-law Helen.

This is not fiction. You will either spend eternity in heaven or hell. You may make fun of this now, ridicule it and try to forget it. I can guarantee you one thing: You will think about it when you bend over double with a heart attack, your vision dims and your breath goes away. If the doctor tells you that you have cancer and three months to live, you will think about this. If you have a peaceful deathbed and your family gathers around to watch you die, you will think of this. I would rather you consider me harsh now and thank God in eternity that you listened to me now, than to like me now and burn in hell forever. It is that straightforward.

You would do well to take this seriously. I have visited with businessmen on their deathbeds. Eternity is breathing down their necks. Their heart weakens. Their breathing becomes shallow. Their palms are perspiring. Guess what? Not one of them has ever said, "I wish I could spend one more day at the office." None of them has ever pled for time to make one more deal. They are suddenly aware that they must prepare for eternity.

You should read this book with the same intensity you would read it if your physician had just told you that you had six months to live. It can change forever your destiny and that of those around you.

Chapter Two

Fake Funerals and Perjured Preachers

"We have gathered together here today to honor the memory of Harold Rhodes. His wife Betty and son Henry survive him. I want you to know, Harold died and went to hell."

How many times have you heard a funeral begin with those words? I can guess. I have never said those words nor have you heard those words at a funeral. We talk about hell generally, theoretically and theologically. But when it comes to identifying a given person who died and went there, we balk. We just can't seem to bring ourselves to be that honest at a funeral.

In that regard, I need to ask your forgiveness. In fact, all of us in the ministry need to ask your forgiveness. I lied. We all lied. Please do not judge us too harshly or too quickly. There is a reason that we fake it at funerals and perjure ourselves as preachers. We want to comfort people. It is a professional expectation. We believe what Paul wrote when he prayed, *that we may be able to comfort those who are in any trouble, with the comfort with which we ourselves are comforted by God* (2 Corinthians 1:4). We want to bring consolation to people who are grieving. But actually, we have lied.

Consider this. A man who in his lifetime never showed any interest in God or the things of God, is lying in a casket. He loved his business, his golf game, his country club, his lake house and his cars. So we preach at the funeral that he was a great businessman. We remember how much he enjoyed golf. We recognize his membership in the Rotary or the country club, but at the same time we totally avoid the obvious. This man had no interest whatsoever in anything remotely related to God, Christ, the gospel or even the church. We picture him sitting and singing praises to God forever, when he could not stand to be in church one hour a week praising God. We conclude that he is with the holy apostles and the saints of the ages forever, when he would rather have been in the card room at the club smoking cigars, drinking gin and playing poker. Before you think I am exaggerating, just remember some of the funerals you have attended.

At one funeral the preacher waxed on and on with soaring eloquence about the deceased's devotion to his family, his church and his God. After about thirty minutes of this, his widow whispered to one of the sons, "Go lift the lid of that casket and see if that is your father in there." Some families certainly must have felt that way at memorial services.

We find shallow solace in the flimsy memory that thirty-five years earlier a man walked down the aisle in a church, filled out a card, was immersed in water or sprinkled and then for the rest of his life never gave any evidence whatsoever that Christ had changed his life in any way. We preach him into a heaven where redeemed saints will spend eternity singing the praises of a Jesus who was a total stranger to the man.

Such preaching reminds me of the story of an ineffective surgeon. The surgeon was famous. He conducted many operations. When patients were wheeled into the operating room, the surgeon and his assistants were immaculately robed in the finest scrubs. The operating room itself was state-of-the-art. The hospital was famous as was the surgeon. After the patient was anesthetized, the surgeon would make a few futile passes over the skin of the patient with a sharp scalpel. Yet a strange thing happened. When the patients were wheeled out of the operating room to the ICU, they never got better. In fact, they died. The surgeon remained famous. He kept on operating. Patients kept on dying. Nothing was ever said.

Finally a first-year intern, a rather dull and plodding student, dared to state the obvious. No incision was ever made. The scalpel never cut the skin. The whole procedure in the operating room was a mere charade. A highly trained man in a beautiful gown, wielding a sharp knife, never really cut the patient open. Patient after patient never got any better.

Is this not exactly what happens in most pulpits Sunday after Sunday? Highly trained ministers, some in beautiful doctoral robes, others in Armani suits, stand in famous institutions with the Sword of the Spirit in their hands, but never really use it to cut. They make a futile pass over the congregation with some platitudes about how to win over worry or how to manage finances, but they never state the obvious. People are never warned. They are never upset. They are never challenged with eternity. They are never cut. They leave church, go to the restaurant, go home and fall asleep watching a ball game, but they were never cut with the Word of God. They were never warned that they were going to hell without a relationship with God through Jesus Christ.

Why is it that in our churches the only time people ever hear about eternity is during a funeral service? Why do they never hear about hell at the 11 o'clock hour on Sunday morning?

For one reason, the movie industry has done its best to present a convenient universalism. In the Hollywood version of eternity, everybody goes to heaven. Movies such as *Heaven Can Wait, Always* and *Ghost* send everybody to heaven. And what a heaven it is! Even Burt Reynolds played God. Never in the Hollywood version of eternity does anyone ever die and go to hell.

There are much broader cultural reasons for the absence of anything like a straight word about hell. Hell is an embarrassment in the church today because of several factors. Consider them:

1. **Cultural pluralism.** Christians in general, and evangelical Christians in particular, are far more educated and well traveled than ever before. We have been to college. We have taken trips to Europe and the Far East. We have seen secularism in England, Islam in the Middle East, Buddhism in Japan and Hinduism in India. We are overwhelmed with the religious diversity in the world around us. We are broad-minded. We are eclectic in our thinking. We gradually forget the sharp distinction between the teachings of Jesus Christ and the platitudes of other world religions. We lower the bar. We

relax our thinking. We do not want to deal with the exclusive and absolute truth claims of Jesus Christ, who demanded total allegiance to Him as the only road to heaven. We forget His statement, *I am the way, the truth, and the life. No man cometh to the Father, except through me* (John 14:6).

We forget that truth is truth in every realm. Just because a Buddhist does not believe two plus two equals four does not change that truth. Just because a Moslem refuses to believe in gravity does not cause gravity to lose its force. We would consider that kind of thinking foolish and illogical.

We should remember that the truth about heaven and hell is not a relative truth. Some of us think that hell used to be the truth but no longer is the truth. We consider hell to be a recollection of Dante's *Inferno* that scared the serfs into submission in the High Middle Ages, but not a reality for an Internet world. It just does not fit into our relativistic view of modern culture.

2. **Theological liberalism.** Beginning with the Enlightenment and continuing through the twentieth century, the church has been assaulted by theological liberalism. In its broadest definition, such liberalism sits in judgment on the

Word of God. It determines what is inspired and what is not inspired. It is a Dalmatian theology. It declares that the Bible is inspired in spots and the liberal theologian is inspired to pick the spots.

One of liberalism's high priests was Rudolph Bultmann, the German theologian who taught at the University of Marburg. Bultmann concluded that modern humans were unwilling to accept the Bible's version of a miraculous universe. So Bultmann "de-mythologized" the Bible. He wanted to keep the ethical core of Jesus' teachings while ridding it of the miraculous husk around that kernel. One of the first things to disappear in his program was the very notion of an eternal hell. Such pagan thought had to be eradicated from the Bible. This eradication has taken two primary forms in the liberal theological world.

One form of theological liberalism is universalism. The theory of universalism declares that every person will go to heaven. It makes no difference what that person believed or how that person lived. The child rapist who is executed will go to heaven just as quickly as the missionary who died for Jesus on a foreign field. Universalism is a mushy, comfortable, vague, hazy hope that everybody will go to heaven forever. The oft spoken phrase, "we are all God's children," epitomizes this false concept.

A more popular view has emerged among theological liberals and has even found currency among some evangelical scholars. That view is called "annihilationism" or "conditional immortality." This view considers that every individual will be raised at the last day to appear before God. Every life will be reviewed, and only those who trusted in Christ or "lived for value" will enter into eternity. After judgment, those who did not pass the test will be obliterated, annihilated, and cease to live as conscious individuals. There will be for them a moment of judgment, a blast of fire and then nothingness forever.

These two views are accommodating to the cultural pluralism and the theological relativism of the modern mind. They represent the modern world's attempt to rationalize the unpleasant reality of an eternal hell.

None of these views change the nature of reality. I may stop believing the sun rises in the east, but that does not change the fact. I may stand by Niagara Falls and deny that there is a roar of water, but that does not change the fact. I may look over into the pit of hell and deny its reality, but that does not change the fact.

We're told that every sixty minutes 4,417 people go out into eternity. Just think, that is roughly seventy-four people every minute of every day! You will most definitely die if Jesus tarries. Hebrews 9:27 states the truth for all time: *And as it is appointed for men to die once, but after this is the judgment.* You have a date with deity, an appointment with the Almighty. Hollywood nor the media will determine the nature of that date. Neither George Burns or Burt Reynolds will be God. The Almighty God, maker of heaven and earth, will be God and His son Jesus your judge.

Modern American Christians simply refuse to believe what the Bible says about hell. Jesus Christ said more about hell than anyone else in the Bible. Someone has noted that the greatest sandstorm in history will be when believers blow the dust off their Bibles. One man actually told me he had placed his mother's Bible by his bed when she died. He stated, "If the St. James version was good enough for her, it is good enough for me." I wonder how often he had picked up the "St. James" version of the Bible?

This book contains a simple message on a serious subject. Only a foolish person would die without the facts on eternal destiny. The only solid information we have on the subject of heaven and hell is the Word of God. The overwhelming majority of Americans, some 71%, believe in a heaven, while less than 13% believe in an eternal hell, and none of them believe they are going there. This statistic in and of itself shows the great confusion about the nature of both.

Suppose with me for a moment that there is only a 10% chance that the Bible is correct in its clear teaching about an eternal hell. What if there was only a one in ten chance that it is right? If you were waiting at the airport to catch a plane and saw that one out of every ten planes taking off crashed and burned, what would you do? It might be the first, the fifth or the ninth plane, but one out of every ten went down at the end of the runway in a great ball of fire. Would you fly? I doubt you would fly at all. If there was a 10% chance that your plane would not reach its destination, you would not dare get on that plane. You should approach this book with the same caution. If there was only a 10% chance that there is an eternal hell, should you not consider it seriously? Should you not seek the truth from God Himself?

Dateline: 1960

Betty Rhodes sat in the congregation at the funeral home while the minister gave the eulogy of Harold Rhodes. The liberal preacher intoned, "Harold Rhodes was a pillar of this community. He had perfect attendance at the Rotary for 30 years. He was a 20-year member at the Bent Shrub Country Club. You will notice by the presence of his lodge brothers on the front row that this was a man who was truly a man among men...."

Betty listened to this ministerial drivel, and, even in her grief, regretted that the minister did not warn the congregation that those who died like her husband would go straight to hell.

She grieved for Harold with a grief that was beyond mere grief. As a godly woman, who knew the eternal destiny of those who died with Christ and those who died without Him, she had the most reverent fear for the fate of her husband. She quietly prayed, through her tears, that the preacher would warn Harold's drinking buddies of the eternal fate of those who died without Christ. Yet the preacher droned on and on about Harold's life membership in the state university's alumni club, his total dedication to the motorcycle club and his trophy winning stint on his bowling team. Poor Betty could not believe her ears.

"Harold never missed a charity chili cook-off," the minister whined, as if he had pronounced Harold worthy of the same honor as a missionary. Even Harold's lost friends wondered who in the world the preacher was talking about.

Harold was in no such state of amusement. The moment he doubled over with a heart attack while mowing his back yard, he sensed something more ominous than the heart attack. At first, Harold lay on the green grass, clawing it with his hands as if he could thereby hang on to his life. His self-propelled mower ran into the nearby fence and continued to whirl and gurgle in place. Harold felt the life going out of him. Indeed, in a moment he was looking down at his dead body on the ground. Harold wanted to go back. He wanted to finish the yard, go in and have a beer and watch the sports show on ESPN like he always did. Instead, Harold was going away from everything he had ever known. Without saying a word, two enormous winged creatures carried Harold far away from his family, his mower, his yard and

Normal, Ohio.

More quickly than he could have imagined, Harold stood in a different world. He was in a place that was dark, hot and lonely. The angelic beings pushed him through what looked like a door and he fell through an abyss, a great gulf. Harold heard unearthly screams and felt a searing heat. A cackling demonic creature lunged at him and threw him into a fiery pit. Harold screamed, writhed and begged somebody to help him. A leering demonic gargoyle spat on him and declared, "You will never get out of here. It will only get darker and hotter." Harold screamed an unearthly scream and tried to run out of the darkness. The further he ran the hotter and darker it became.

By the time the minister was bragging on old Harold, he had run so far into hell that he felt only darkness and heat and distance from God, but most of all, isolation. Harold was all alone. Where was the party he and his buddies used to joke about? How many times had Harold laughed and said, "Yeah, when I end up in hell we'll all have a big party." Harold found out he had been wrong all those times. No friends! No party! Harold was completely, totally alone!

Chapter Three

Hell: The Suffering

The scorching sun is beating down on the muscles and sinews of His exposed back, which was shredded by the Roman whip the night before. Lacerated, tormented by insects, bruised by beatings and blinded by sweat, He carries a Roman Cross through the streets of Jerusalem. The spittle and abuse from the crowd sting more than the swarming flies.

When He reaches His destination, the base of a barren, skull-like hill outside the city walls, He is told to lay down the instrument of His own execution. His hands are stretched out on the wood and nails are pounded through them. His feet are likewise pinned to the wood with iron nails. The cross is lifted up high and dropped into a prepared hole in the rocky soil. The jolt rips through His body with a hellish pain. He hangs in the sun for six hours. His friends abandon Him. The crowd jeers at Him. Even the Supreme Court of the day scoffs at Him from beneath His Cross. Dehydrated, bleeding to death, blistered by the Judean sun, He dies. A sword is rammed into Him and breaks the pericardium around His heart. Water and blood flow out of His side. Jesus Christ is crucified. The Son of God is dead.

No more poignant picture of absolute suffering exists than the death of the Son of God by crucifixion. God sent His only begotten Son to the Cross for the salvation of humanity and of every human who would receive Him. The world gave the infinite, perfect sacrifice of God its most degrading death. The world will go to hell for that.

Why will people experience the suffering of hell's torments? Will they feel the pain of hell because of lying? Lying is deceitful, injurious and ruinous to careers and reputations. But people will not go to hell because they lied.

Will people go to hell because of adultery? There may be no greater pain in life than the pain of adultery, the breaking of vows that inevitably result in the breaking of hearts. But people do not go to hell because of adultery.

Murder takes the life of another person, whether it is the murder of a fetus in the womb or the murder of a child by an insane rapist. Do people go to hell because of murder? No, people do not go to hell because of murder.

People go to hell because they reject the suffering sacrifice of the Lord Jesus Christ on the Cross. The price of rejecting an infinite sacrifice is an infinite suffering.

In short, the pain of hell is the eternal retribution of rejecting the infinite pain of the perfect sacrifice of the Son of God. If you reject what He did in enduring the most excruciating penalty in history, you will go to hell for that.

Hell is a place of suffering. *And being in torments in Hades, he lifted up his eyes...* (Luke 16:23). The rich man of Jesus' parable cried out, *I am in agony in this flame* (Luke 16:24). The man begged that the leper who lay outside his gate in his earthly life now come and touch his tongue with just one drop of water for that most slight relief. Jesus paints a picture of total and permanent torture and torment in a place called hell.

One of the greatest difficulties of the liberal theologians who love Jesus but reject hell is the grave truth that *Jesus said more about hell than anyone else.* The same tenderhearted Lord who healed the diseased, gave sight to the blind, hearing to the deaf and freed the demon-possessed from their demons was the same Lord who gave the most vivid pictures of hell in the New Testament. Jesus said more about hell than did the Apostle Paul. He repeatedly gave sobering warnings of the eternal nature of torment in hell. You cannot have the Jesus of the New Testament without His teachings about hell. If you doubt His teachings about hell, you had just as well doubt the story of His crucifixion and resurrection.

The person who doubts the existence of hell must deny the Word of God or consider that Jesus was simply mistaken or that He deliberately misled people. If Jesus was mistaken, He was not the perfect Son of God and we have no business believing anything He said about God. We should all go back to the synagogue, which was the last revelation of God before Jesus. If Jesus deliberately misled humanity about the existence of hell, He has perpetrated an incredible fraud on the human race. He does not deserve the name Lord and should not be worshiped if He deceived humanity about the existence of a terrible place called hell.

The only other possibility is the invention of hell by the early church and the fraudulent placement of the teaching about hell on the lips of Jesus. This is the conclusion of the modern, so-called "Jesus Seminar." This outlandish group of liberal university scholars considers that most of the Gospels are an invention of the early church, including their teaching about hell. If this were true, then we can rely on *nothing* in the New Testament. If it were possible that Matthew, Mark, Luke and John invented stories out of the blue and placed them on the lips of Jesus, there is no basis for our faith whatsoever.

To the contrary, the best evangelical scholars have discovered through painstaking research that the earliest church carefully treasured the words of Jesus and preserved them with great care. The *ipsissima verba*, the very words of Jesus, were treasured by the holy apostles and the church fathers for centuries. They would not dare change a fragment of what He said.

My friend, you are up against an awesome truth. Jesus taught the reality of hell because hell is a reality. He could not have been the Son of God and the Savior of the world without telling us the truth about the awful consequence of rejecting His sacrifice.

When your heart takes its last beat, you are going to awaken in one of two eternal dimensions. You will wake up in the glorious presence of Almighty God and His eternal Son amidst the saints of the ages and myriads of angels, or you are going to wake up all alone in hell. Yes, I wrote all alone. One of C. S. Lewis's greatest insights was penned in his book about hell, *The Great Divorce*, possibly the greatest book ever written about hell. Lewis confronts the usual sinner's comfort about hell that all of the sinner's friends will be there. This false thinking makes hell a sort of perpetual good ol' boys' club.

Demolishing this argument, he shows how hell will be a lonely place of people infinitely distant from one another. Part of the punishment of hell will be the loneliness. Do not expect you will be in a great crowd like a sports bar on Saturday night. You will be tormented and alone.

Your last heartbeat and your last breath will not be the end of your existence. When God breathed the breath of life into the nostrils of Adam, He infused in Adam and into every individual who has lived since Adam, an eternal spirit. The image of God within us, even the most fractured image of God in the most deplorable sinner, remains and lasts forever. There is an infinite chasm between the lowest, worst, miserable sinful human and the highest ape. Humans are instilled with eternal existence. You cannot will that away. You are eternal and will exist somewhere for eternity. That is part of what it means to be created in the image of God.

The preacher who speaks or writes of hell is accused of using scare tactics. He is rejected for being manipulative. Liberal theologians condescend to him as if he were a mutated specimen from another era. Nothing could be further from the truth. The authentic biblical preacher who warns people of hell is warning them of a serious hazard. He understands that it would be a tragedy for them to be misinformed or uninformed concerning the nature of eternal existence.

It is difficult for a dedicated physician to tell a long-time patient that he or she has cancer. But what physician would refuse to give the obvious warning just because the truth was hard to hear? A legal counselor must sometimes educate a client with hard truths about breaking the law. What kind of attorney would not warn a client of the consequences of violating the law? An accountant must often warn clients against shady tax deductions or sloppy bookkeeping that could lead to an audit. What kind of accountant would refuse to do this and only tell what the client wanted to hear? Responsible professionals in every discipline tell their clients the truth.

As the Surgeon General of the United States has warned that smoking cigarettes will likely kill you physically, it is my absolute responsibility to tell you what you do not want to hear. I have no choice in that matter. My calling and my obligation to you binds me. I would be like a pilot who knew that a plane was unsafe, but still boarded the passengers in defiance of what they needed to know.

It is an impossibility to describe hell. No one has been to hell and come back to tell about it. There are books in print today reporting to tell the story of those who have had an "out of body" experience in which they visited hell and returned. I am not buying into that philosophy. We must never rely on personal anecdotes where there is biblical truth to certify what is said. For example, I believe the story of Noah's Ark whether someone finds the ark in Turkey or not. In the same way, I do not have to interview someone who has literally been to hell and back to validate my belief in hell. In fact, Jesus addressed that very point when he said, *If they do not hear Moses and the prophets, neither will they be persuaded though one rise from the dead* (Luke 16:31).

What is hell like? Is it a literal fire? Dr. Billy Graham has been asked that repeatedly. Dr. Graham responds that he does not know, but that every symbol in the Bible stands for a reality that is stronger than the symbol. If the Bible tells us that hell is fire, then the reality must be worse than the symbol.

Have you ever burned your finger? You know the excruciating pain of a simple burn on one finger. I am aware of a Washington man who was burned over 99% of his body. People can barely stand to look at him. He cannot begin to explain the pain that he has suffered. There is no way a person can explain that kind of pain. It is beyond comprehension. Yet the suffering of hell will be of a burning nature more severe than that.

Jesus repeatedly used the Aramaic term *Gehenna* when He referred to hell. The people of His day understood this term to be a reference to the Valley of Hinnom outside the Dung Gate of the New Testament City of Jerusalem. The refuse and garbage from the city was carried out the Dung Gate and dumped into the Valley of Hinnom. It was a place of perpetual fire and vermin. The stench, the maggots, the fire and the garbage conjured up the image of a terrible destiny. The gentle Lord Jesus used this to describe the destiny of those who died rejecting His sacrifice on the Cross.

What an awful image! Hell is something of a cosmic garbage dump. What would it be like to find oneself forever in a place of such torment that the Son of God Himself could only compare it to a garbage dump? This is sobering language indeed. In the parable of the Rich Man and the Beggar, Jesus says twice that the rich man was in agony and another time that he was in torment.

C. S. Lewis in *The Great Divorce* suggests an unusual insight on the subject of hell. The book is a fictional trip to heaven undertaken by some residents from hell. When the men and women from hell arrive in heaven, they find that they cannot stand anything about it. First, the green grass itself is like spikes to their feet. It is too real. The light is too bright and they complain that it sears their eyes. The liquid water is solid under their feet and they cannot drink it. Heaven is simply too *real* for them to stand it. That is, for folks bound for hell, heaven itself would be hell. Why should a person who cannot stand an hour singing hymns in church want to listen to a heavenly choir forever? Why should someone whose deeds are done in darkness expect to enjoy a setting where everything forever is done in the light? Heaven would be hell to those whose destiny is hell.

I have been asked on numerous occasions, "Why would a loving God send anyone to an eternal hell?" The fact is, God does not send anyone to hell! God sent His only Son to the Cross in order that no one would have to experience hell. You either accept or reject the mighty deed of Christ on the Cross. Those who reject the suffering of the eternal Son of God will populate hell. He paid an infinite price so that we could escape the destination of hell. If we refuse that infinite price that was paid, there is an infinite hell to experience. The choice is yours. God hangs the heaviest weights on the thin wire of decision.

Dateline: 1960

More than anything in the world, Harold Rhodes wanted to come back to warn his son Henry. Harold had doted on Henry. He spent hours playing catch with him. He showed him how to shoulder a shotgun and lead a dove. He demonstrated how to field dress a deer. He had cheered Henry at T-ball games and on the high school football team. Harold had not, however, told Henry about the Lord Jesus Christ. He had not warned Henry of the consequences of rejecting Christ. Harold had not told Henry about hell.

While Harold burned in hell, he wanted more than anything else to warn Henry about that awful place. But he could not do so. He screamed the name of his son in the halls of hell, but the scream fell on no ears at all. Harold could not go back and he could not tell Henry. Henry had churches all around him, Christian friends and, like Harold, would have a Christian wife. If he would not listen to them, it would make no difference if Harold could go back.

Chapter Four

Hell: The Separation

...between us and you there is a great gulf fixed, so that those who want to pass from here to you cannot, nor can those from there cross to us (Luke 16:26).

All of us want a second chance. It is deeply imbedded into human nature to desire another opportunity. Every student who has failed wants a second chance. Every gambler that has lost his money desires another game. Football teams are notorious for saying, "Wait until next year." Boxers want another round. Racers want another lap. We do not like absolute finality.

For that reason humanity finds the finality of hell a difficult concept to grasp. The Bible teaches our eternal fate is sealed forever the moment we die. There is no second chance in life. When we die, our eternal destiny is fixed.

There is something in mere human rationality

that reacts against that. This has resulted in a great deal of creativity on the part of certain theologians. Entire branches of the Christian church hold to the existence of an interim holding place, a post-mortem spiritual refinery. It is usually called purgatory and almost always belongs to a theology of salvation by works.

The theology of purgatory works somewhat like a bank account. A person who dies with more bad deeds than good deeds may be sentenced to purgatory for a length of time determined by the bank account balance of bad versus good deeds. Additional good deeds may be deposited to his account by living relatives or friends. Reciting certain prayers or giving donations to the church does this. Sometimes it is supposed that departed saints in heaven have so many good deeds in their heavenly bank accounts that they could contribute some to the account of the soul in purgatory. When sufficient rehabilitation has taken place, the soul in purgatory enters into heaven.

One of the motivating causes of the Protestant Reformation was the Catholic Church's teaching about purgatory. A certain monk, John Tetzel, was raising money for the most recent building program of the church, St. Peter's Basilica in Rome. He uttered a famous line of poetry in western history: "The moment a coin in the coffer rings, another soul from purgatory springs." In this very mercantile approach to personal salvation, Tetzel sold an exit from purgatory for a departed loved one in exchange for a contribution to the building program of the church. This so disgusted an Augustinian monk named Martin Luther that he protested this teaching and thus began the Protestant Reformation. Luther found no biblical evidence whatsoever for the human invention of a halfway house for a second chance.

The doctrine of a second chance, based on purgatory, misunderstands the nature of personal salvation and divine grace. Works cannot save you in this life, no less in the life to come: *For by grace you have been saved through faith, and that not of yourselves; it is the gift of God, not of works, lest any man should boast* (Ephesians 2:8-9). Personal merit has nothing to do with salvation, either in this life or the life to come. Paul makes it clear for all the ages when he writes, *by the deeds of the law no flesh will be justified in His sight* (Romans 3:20). If works will not save you in this life on earth, neither your works nor someone else's will save you in the eternity to come. All salvation is by grace extended in this present life.

Those who believe in a second chance do not understand the nature of salvation by grace. God has made you an offer so good that it is a reflection on Him and His character for you to turn it down. It is literally an offer that is so good that it is only made once. That God would send His only begotten Son to die for you is an offer that you have only one lifetime to accept. Actually, it would be gracious enough of God if He gave you one day or one month to consider the death of His Son for you. Instead, God gives you an entire lifetime to accept the death of His Son for your sins and the sins of the world. If you choose not to trust and receive Jesus Christ as your Lord and Savior in your natural lifetime, you will have no more time to do so.

We consider this to be the case in natural human life. Some offers deserve to be accepted when they are offered, or not at all. Suppose an affluent man loves a woman who is poor, downtrodden, angry, alienated, isolated and hateful. He seeks her out, loves her purely and treats her generously. He builds a beautiful home for her. He makes every provision for her safety and comfort, but she rejects him.

Dateline: 1960
Meanwhile in Hell

Harold Rhodes never believed in anything he could not see. Although he would never have used the word, he was a strict empiricist. The world of religion, art, philosophy and anything else other than working at the tire plant near Normal meant nothing to him.

One can imagine Harold's surprise, then,

when he woke up in hell. He sensed first of all the most desolate feeling of alienation and separation he had ever felt. It was the same feeling he had felt when he shipped off to World War II and left home for the first time, but it was ten thousand times worse than that. He felt utterly, totally, completely, and desperately alone.

It never dawned on Harold that hell would be so lonely. He had often thought to himself, "If there is a hell, all of my friends will be there," and he chuckled to himself when he thought that. Harold was not close to anybody. What Harold did not know was that C. S. Lewis was right when he described hell as a place where people are always getting farther and farther away from one another.

Harold missed Betty. Little did he know that the day would come that he would look across the great gulf and see Betty and his daughter-in-law Helen rejoicing in the presence of the Lord Jesus Christ.

Harold looked around in hell and saw nothing but darkness and felt nothing but heat. But then Harold looked up. His heart — if he had had one — stopped. Above him in a rainbow of light was the throne of Almighty God. Beside it he saw the Person he had despised in his life, the Lord Jesus Christ. Since Harold was spiritually in hell but awaiting the Great White Throne for his final and total judgment, he had an ominous feeling that he would stand in the presence of that One on the Throne. A fear surpassing anything he had felt in his life overtook him. He suddenly remembered the life of profanity, obscenity, lewdness, secrecy and everything else that Betty had never known about.

Betty had been a rock, the stronger of the two of them. He knew he would never see her again. This thought sunk him deeper into fear and despair. But then he thought of Henry. Henry should not come here. He did not want his son in this awful, dark, hot, lonely place. He had a sense that even if his son had been there, he would never see him again.

Harold began to wail in the darkness, "Don't let Henry come here!" He pleaded, begged, cried and screamed. No one heard and no one cared. When he tried to look around him, his eyes saw nothing but darkness. When he looked up he saw the Throne of God. When he looked behind, he saw his past with regret. When he looked ahead, he saw only despair. Harold did not know it, but Dante had written centuries before the words over the door of hell, "Despair of hope, all ye that enter here." Harold had never heard of Dante, but he was living the reality of eternal separation from God.

Chapter Five

The Great Snatching Away

But of that day and hour no one knows, not even the angels of heaven, but My Father only (Matthew 24:36).

It was something that had never happened in the history of aviation. The sleek, needle-nosed aircraft had a perfect safety record. For a generation, the rich and the famous, in a hurry to get across the Atlantic, had paid the premium to fly on the Concorde. Yet on July 25, 2000, in the village of Gonesse, France, a Concorde crashed, taking the lives of all on board and four on the ground. No one thought it could happen.

On board the ill-fated flight, the excited passengers were headed for New York City. From New York City they would fly to Florida to embark on a Caribbean cruise. The experienced crew and the worldly passengers expected everything to go as it had always gone. Yet this time it was different. The same sophisticated passengers had done the same thing in the same way many times. But their same plans had a different ending.

The Lord Jesus Christ spoke of His stealthy, sudden return to snatch away His church in the same terms:

> *But as the days of Noah were, so also will the coming of the Son of Man be. For as in the days before the flood, they were eating and drinking, marrying and giving in marriage, until the day that Noah entered the ark, and did not know until the flood came and took them all away, so also will the coming of the Son of Man be* (Matthew 24:37-39).

The generation of Noah and the generation of the new millennium have something in common. They both believe in *uniformity* rather than *catastrophe*. That is, they believe that the world will go on just as it has always gone on. They laugh at spiritual warnings, sneer at presumed-ignorant preachers and scoff at quiet Christians who warn that Christ will suddenly return for His own. They continue their round of daily dining, beverage consuming and planning for a life of marriage, peace and tranquility. They believe that the round of life, whether at the country club or the bowling alley, will always be as it is.

Noah's generation experienced the sudden, sobering reality that this lifestyle does not happen in a world ruled by God rather than human expectations. Right up until the catastrophe occurred, Noah's generation continued the unimpeded round of normal life. Then, one day, a reveler felt a splash of water on his arm and then another on his face. He'd never before seen or felt rain.

"Maybe we ought to cancel the party and check this out," he said.

"Let's go ahead with the party," his friend countered.

And so they did, right up until the moment Noah entered the ark, God closed the door, and the party-goers remarked that the rain did not seem to be stopping.

Turn Out the Lights; the Party's Over

Remember Dandy Don Meredith and the early days of Monday Night Football with Meredith, Howard Cosell and Frank Gifford? When the game was out of reach, Dandy Don would croon the tune, "Turn out the lights; the party's over." In a real sense the United States of America, land of the Pilgrim Fathers and a haven for persecuted

European Christians who wanted a new start, has been in a party since the 1960s. Americans have thought that the party would go on forever. Peace, prosperity, unimpeded economic growth, unfettered personal liberty and perpetual self-absorption have marked the Modern and Postmodern worlds. Yet deep in the hearts of aging baby boomers there is a growing sense that something is about to happen. And they are right.

In the economy of God, the next thing on the agenda of heaven is the coming of the Lord Jesus Christ for His own. The earliest Christian writers called this the *Parousia,* a Greek term which means "the being alongside." The term was used technically for the visit of a king to his realm. The next epochal event recorded on the eternal Palm Pilot will be the sudden visit of King Jesus to snatch away His Church. The Church has come to call this the *Rapture.* That word in Latin, *raptere,* referred to snatching something away. For example, a lady is walking down the street with her handbag on her arm and out of nowhere a thief runs by and rips the bag away. This is what the Rapture is, a snatching away. The next thing on heaven's timetable is the great snatching away of the Church.

The Rapture will have radically different outcomes for the saved and the lost. For the saved the Rapture will be inexpressible joy and celebration.

Those Christians who have died and been careful-ly put away in earthen graves or marble mau-soleums will find their disembodied spirits sudden-ly restored to their resurrected bodies. Christians who have died are spiritually present with the Lord but they are not yet completed without their Resurrection bodies. Paul makes it clear that the disembodied state of being-with-Christ is not the perfect intention of God (2 Corinthians 5:2). The saints of the ages will come forth from seas and cat-acombs, vast city cemeteries and little, lost country graveyards. There will be hallelujahs in the air as grandparents, parents and children see one another in their perfect, eternal, spiritual bodies.

On the other hand, those who died outside of Christ will simply remain bodily in the same dusty, decomposing and disintegrating state they have endured in the grave. While their spirits are con-sciously tortured in the flames of hell, their bodies will await the final judgment of God known as the Great White Throne Judgment when all the lost of the ages will stand before God.

It is interesting to contemplate whether the disembodied spirits of the lost dead in hell will observe the Rapture and the Resurrection of the believers. In all likelihood they will. What remorse, regret, anguish, screams of lost opportu-nity and wails of dread will fill the halls of hell when the disembodied spirits of the lost dead observe the Resurrection of the righteous, saved dead! The realization that they have missed forever the opportunity to experience such bliss will then penetrate the stony hearts of the impenitent dead. They will stare into the deep abyss of their own doom, dreading the certain judgment to come. That horror will be amplified as the catastrophe of rejecting Christ settles in and they see saved family members receiving resurrection bodies.

There's Going to be a Meeting in the Air

Immediately after the Resurrection of the righteous dead, the living Christians on earth will experience an incredible transformation. Wherever they are and whatever they are doing, they will suddenly begin to ascend into the clouds of heaven. They will levitate by the command of God Himself. As they are en route, they will find their bodies being transformed suddenly. Paul declares that this will happen, *in the twinkling of an eye* (1 Corinthians 15:52). The Greek word *atomos* gives us our English word "atom" and suggests the least divisible amount of anything. Paul states that in the least divisible amount of time, in time so sudden that it cannot be divided any more, we will be changed into our new spiritual bodies.

Consider the remarkable experience this shall present. Old men, wracked with arthritis or stooped with time, will suddenly find themselves renewed, youthful, vigorous and energetic. The Christian quadriplegic will suddenly leap from the wheelchair and experience the freedom of mobility. The blind Christians cowering in some corner will see the bright beauty of the appearing of the Christ. There's going to be a meeting in the air! The joy, bliss, ecstasy and wonder of it defy all description.

The When of the Rapture

There are several views about the timing of this incredible event. I believe the Scriptures teach a Pre-Tribulational view. This view simply means this event will take place before (hence the prefix, pre) the world is thrust into the seven-year tribulation period. Some have suggested that those who choose to believe this do so out of fear, a sort of pie-in-the-sky mentality. In other words, they say believing this is comforting to their souls and calming to their anxiety. It is rather strange they would make this accusation considering what the Word of God itself states. The apostle Paul says it this way:

For the Lord himself will descend from heaven with a shout, with the voice of the archangel, and with the trumpet of God. And the dead in Christ will rise first. Then we who are alive and remain shall be caught up together with them in the clouds, to meet the Lord in the air. And thus we shall always be with the Lord. Wherefore COMFORT one another with these words (1 Thessalonians 4:16-18). (Emphasis mine.)

It is comforting and calming to know in one's heart that as Jesus said, *In the world you will have tribulation* (John 16:33), but that THE TRIBULATION (Matthew 24:22) is not for the believer.

In fact, the only position regarding the Rapture that fits with Scripture completely is the Pre-Tribulational position. This teaching fits if one applies the golden rule of interpretation: when the plain sense of Scripture makes sense, seek no further sense, lest you end up with nonsense. In addition, the Pre-Tribulational position makes perfect sense when we consider that Jesus likened our relationship to Him as the groom and we, the saved, as the bride (see my book *Seven Signs of the Second Coming of Christ* for a complete treatment on this subject). I ask you, what groom takes his bride, puts her through unimaginable horror and judgment, judgment in which 50% of the world's population dies, and then says, "Okay, now I will take you to be my bride"? That idea not only sounds ridiculous, it is ridiculous! The Bible states, *For God did not appoint us to wrath, but to obtain salvation through our Lord Jesus Christ, who died for us, that whether we wake or sleep, we should live together with Him. Therefore comfort each other, and edify one another, just as ye also are doing* (1 Thessalonians 5:9-11).

There are others who believe in a Mid-Tribulational position. These folks believe the saved, the Church, will be left on earth during the first three and one-half years of the tribulation. The disciples of this position make a sharp distinction between the Tribulation and the Great Tribulation. This teaching then has the Rapture occurring in the middle (hence, mid) of the tribulation. I strongly disagree with this. The Scriptures teach that *But of that day and hour no man knows, not even the angels of heaven, but my Father only* (Matthew 24:36). The beginning of THE TRIBULATION is when the nation of Israel enters into a peace agreement with the coming one-world government (Daniel 2) that allows the Jews to rebuild their Temple in Jerusalem and reinstitute Temple worship and sacrifice (Daniel 9:27). The beginning of THE GREAT TRIBULATION is when the Temple sacrifice is stopped, or taken away, and the abomination of desolation (an image of the antichrist) is erected on a wing of the rebuilt Temple (Daniel 12:11). If the saved were on earth during this time they would know that the day of the coming of Jesus would be exactly 1,290 days. This violates imminency regarding Christ's coming. Furthermore, Jesus told us we are to WATCH for His coming (Matthew 25:13). If we were not raptured before the tribulation began we would be watching for tribulation, not Jesus!

A third view is known as the Post-Tribulational view. Some call this the Yo-Yo position since it has the saved going up in the Rapture and immediately turning around and coming down in the Second Coming. As you might suspect it simply means the Rapture will occur after THE TRIBULATION. This position has the church present on earth during the entire seven-year period. Again, this violates the imminency factor of Christ's return. If we were present on earth during this period we would simply count forward 2,520 days (360 days in a Jewish year times seven years) and add 30 days or one month, and then you have the return of Jesus (Daniel 12:11). In addition this view allows no time in heaven for the Judgment Seat of Christ (Romans 14:10, 2 Corinthians 5:10) or the Marriage Supper of the Lamb (Revelation 19:9).

The Partial-Rapture theory, yet another Rapture position, is a relatively new idea. Without going into detail on this preposterous position, let me say that it is built on shifting sand and lacks a solid biblical foundation. The idea in a nutshell is that only the Spirit-filled, sold-out, dedicated believers will be raptured. The believers who are saved, *so as through fire* (1 Corinthians 3:15) will be left behind to endure the suffering of the tribulation. The proof text for this idea seems to be the passage in Matthew 25:1-13 where Jesus is teaching using a parable of five wise virgins and five foolish ones. The key phrase in this passage are the words in verse 12, *I do not know you*, indicating these foolish ones are not saved. Therefore we can say with certainty that to suggest a division among believers is wrong. As a former pastor there were times I would have liked to have taught this idea. However, being true to Scripture forbade it.

Dateline: 1964
Meanwhile Back at the Cemetery

In 1954 Harold and Betty Rhodes had, at the urging of Harold's mother, purchased two burial plots next to Harold's parents. Many considered Restland Park to be one of the most desirable cemeteries in Normal, Ohio, and the Rhodes naturally wished to be buried near one another. This was an irony in as much as their real destinies would be far apart.

Harold died In 1960. Betty Rhodes had paid a fierce price for disobeying the clear commandment of God that believers should not be married to unbelievers (2 Corinthians 6:14). Even though she was a devout woman, she felt she could somehow avoid the sad realities of living with a lost person. Harold had been a decent husband, except for his opposition to the Lord Jesus Christ and everything related to His church. Whenever Betty wished to expand her involvement in the church program, Harold objected to it so vehemently that she submitted to him quietly.

After Harold died, however, it was as if Betty wished to make up for lost time. For four years she earnestly participated in the entire scope of the church program. She worked in the nursery with little children, joined the handbell group on Wednesday evening and sang with the senior choir on Fridays. In retrospect, Betty came to wish she had withstood Harold's objections over the years. Now she understood the joy involved in an unfettered service to the Lord Jesus Christ.

One fateful day, a drunken driver crashed into Betty's car as she returned from the

Sunday morning services. Just as most people, Betty had not awakened that day with any plans of dying. The Bible often reminds us of its certainty, but as the famous psychiatrist suggested, no man can truly conceive his own death. Betty spoke her last words at the wheel of her crushed car, "Lord Jesus, receive my spirit."

Unbelievably, in the least divisible amount of time, Betty was whisked away from the scene of the crash and in her spirit stood in the midst of the events described in Revelation 3 and 4. There was no pain, remorse, regret, fear or shock about the accident she had just experienced, for now she was in the presence of the Father, Son and Holy Spirit and the saints of the ages, singing the praises of the risen Lord Jesus Christ.

Betty did not see the aftermath of her death on earth. The ambulance took her physical body to the hospital where she was pronounced dead upon arrival. Then her mortal remains were taken to Restland Funeral Home. Along with other family members, her son Henry and daughter-in-law Helen gathered in the state room of the funeral home where the closed casket sat in mute silence at Betty's apparently tragic end.

Helen quietly stood in prayerful composure while Henry wailed, bawled and sobbed all over the room in an uncharacteristic display of emotion. Just four years earlier his father had died and now his mother was gone as well. Henry felt the full weight of his own mortality and an ominous sense that all was not well with him after all.

Helen had often tried to share the Word and will of God with Henry — the fallen nature of the world, the certainty of suffering, the reality of death and eternity. Henry would have nothing of it. He usually left the room, opened a beer and turned on a ball game. Henry even speeded up when he drove by a cemetery at night, like a child afraid of the dark.

Henry excused himself to the men's room to regain his composure. When he came out, he noticed on a nearby table a gospel tract entitled, "Got Life." Just as he picked up the tract, Betty's Bible Study Fellowship leader placed her hand on his shoulder. A remarkable dialogue took place.

"Betty often asked us to pray for you at Bible study," the gentle lady told Henry.

Henry felt a rush of fear, dread and anger welling up inside of him. He choked back his tears and looked into the distance. His dad had warned him about religious people, and he was not about to dishonor old Dad right now.

"Betty so hoped that you would come to the Lord Jesus Christ during her lifetime. She wanted to know that you would be in heaven with her," Dorothy, the Bible study leader pleaded.

Henry turned a pinkish purple. On the one hand he wanted to honor his mother, but on the other hand he liked the irreligious lifestyle of his dad. Besides that, he knew that he was much more ethical in business than many of the men down at the church who had open invoices with his company that they were slow to pay.

Henry politely but firmly told Dorothy, "I have no interest in it at all." Little did Henry realize that he had just sealed his fate in hell.

Future Story
The Next Thing for Betty

After some time, Betty suddenly heard the blast of a great host of trumpets. Then the mighty archangel shouted with a reverberating shout that shook the heavens and the earth.

Majestically, the Father on the Throne turned to his Son, the Lord Jesus Christ, and pronounced, "The last one has been saved. It is time to claim your bride." Then, with a seismic force, all of heaven erupted. The moment for which the Church had awaited for 2,000 years was now at hand. The risen and reigning Lord Jesus Christ stepped out of His invisible glory and on to the clouds of the heavens. In splendor and majesty, power and glory, beauty and light, the returning Lord Jesus Christ moved towards earth. Handel could not have written of it in a thousand oratorios. He opened His arms to welcome home His bride.

Betty looked down on the scene from above. Suddenly she saw her own earthen grave bursting open at Restland Cemetery. In the very act of transformation her physical remains came forth from the grave. Her now glorified body was joined with her soaring spirit. What a meeting in the air! She now had a body like that of her Lord Jesus Christ. Her eyes were not dim, her feet no longer shuffled and her mind was as clear as a rocket scientist. All in an instant and all because of His great power!

At just that moment Betty saw Helen.

Helen had been caught up from the earth along with all of those who were alive at the time of Christ's coming. Both of them looked radiant. They were both 33 years old in appearance, the very age which their Lord appeared to be. They were vibrant, energetic, free, alive forever and like their risen Lord.

Suddenly someone amidst the thousands and thousands being caught up began to sing, "When we've been there ten thousand years...." The entire multitude joined together in singing the old song they had sung so long. But now faith had become sight and it was really happening. *Gloria in excelsis deo.*

Chapter Six

An Appointment We Shall All Keep

For we must all appear before the judgment seat of Christ, that each one may receive the things done in the body, according to what he has done, whether good or bad. Knowing, therefore, the terror of the Lord, we persuade men; but we are well known to God, and I also trust are well known in your consciences (2 Corinthians 5:10-11).

The 1820 presidential inauguration of President Andrew Jackson proved to be most memorable. The great western hero was an outspoken commoner. He pledged that everyone could come to his inauguration party at the White House. When the day came, he was good to his promise. He had invited backwoods friends from his military days. They all came. They came to the White House in their buckskin and coonskin caps. They spit chewing tobacco on the damask furniture coverings. They stood on antiques. They climbed in and out of the windows. It was a wild, indiscriminate crowd that made the aloof Virginians nearby horrified. The Wild West had come to Washington. The only way the officials cleared the house was to place huge tubs of punch on the lawn outside.

It is always humorous when people show up where they are not expected. Andy Jackson's party was just such a time. Almighty God does not expect everybody to show up at the same judgment. In fact, there will be several judgments in the series of divine judicial hearings following the Rapture. The first of these will be for Christians.

The *identity* of those who will appear at the Judgment Seat of Christ is clear. Unlike the Jacksonian party, only those who should be there will be there. Paul makes that clear in 2 Corinthians 5:10 when he indicates that "we" shall be there. The Judgment Seat of Christ is not the place for the judgment of the lost world. That would be a mixture that would lack the appropriateness and the grace that will belong to the great, sobering occasion. For the Judgment Seat of Christ is not to determine the eternal destiny of the rebel lost. It is, rather, a time for the Lord Jesus Christ to review the life of each authentic Christian and to give out the rewards that belong to those believers.

Those present will be Christians.

How inappropriate and unlike God would it be for a Paul to stand in the same line as a Nero, a Luther to stand in the same line as those who threatened his life, a Billy Graham to stand in the same line with a Stalin. That is unthinkable. At the Judgment Seat of Christ only believers shall be present. Only that is appropriate.

Among other reasons, it is appropriate that all the Church of all the ages gathers together at one time and place. Time has swept away one generation of the Church after another. The church militant on earth has never been part of the church triumphant in heaven. God does not see the mighty Church as a series of interrupted starts and stops. He sees His Church as one great Body through the ages. It is appropriate that we should all gather together to receive the rewards for what was done in the flesh for the Lord.

The living lost world must go through the Tribulation and the Great Tribulation. They have no business being at the sobering business of the Judgment Seat of Christ. Their time for judgment is later at the Great White Throne. Part of their judgment is to be on earth during the Tribulation getting exactly what they wanted — a world without the Church and without Christ.

Our presence at the Judgment Seat of Christ is

a *necessity*. We "must" appear there. Have you ever received a summons to be considered for a jury? That is a summons that has the resounding authority of a "must." You may find yourself in real trouble if you do not appear at the courthouse on the day required. Yet there is an appearance for every Christian that is a great "must." We *must* appear at the Judgment Seat of Christ. That is a requirement that none of us shall miss. We may miss church on Sunday night. We may miss visitation. We may miss prayer meeting. None of us will miss the Judgment Seat of Christ.

This is a divine *must*. The word translated "must" is a word in the Greek New Testament that always refers to a divine necessity. The word reflects something that belongs to the nature of the divine expectation and shall indeed happen. It was the word used, for example, by the Lord Jesus Christ when He announced that "the Son of Man *must* go up to Jerusalem..." to face the Cross — and all that it involved. The Cross was a divine necessity in the nature of the case. In the same awesome "oughtness," it is also a divine necessity that believers appear before the Judgment Seat of Christ. It is a part of the divine fabric of the universe that each and every believer will appear before the Judgment Seat of Christ. For God it is a great necessity that every saint appear at the place of judgment for reward in light of faithful service.

God will be no man's debtor. He knows that faithful saints who have spent a lifetime battling the world, the flesh and the devil, deserve a reward. He recognizes that those who have sacrificed on earth deserve their moment in heaven. He takes reward seriously for Christians. In a lower, lesser, lighter way we recognize the necessity of this on earth.

Just off Interstate 77 at Canton, Ohio, is the Pro Football Hall of Fame. Every year a few of the best of the best are enshrined there with a bust and a record of their achievements. The nation demanded and the fans required that we not forget a Johnny Unitas or a Tom Landry or a Walter Payton. There is an obvious *must* that there be somewhere to remember these legends for all they have meant for the game. No one begrudges it. It would be unthinkable that there not be such a place of recognition and honor and celebration.

If that is true on a lower, lesser level how much more is it a necessity on the divine, eternal heavenly level. Shall a Paul or a Wycliffe or a Lottie Moon or a million lesser saints live a life for the Lord Jesus and all of that life be forgotten, unrewarded and unrecognized? No, God shall have a moment of divine necessity when all shall be rewarded.

Some have a problem with the very idea of reward as it relates to the Judgment Seat of Christ. Why should Christians serve God with an eye on reward? Is that a base motive for service? The answer is relatively simple. The reward of the Christian is more of what the Christian always wanted anyway — more of Christ Himself. The reward to a student who practices music faithfully is the ability to play more music. The reward to a scholar who learns a foreign language is the ability to speak that language. The reward of an athlete who trains is excellence in the game. The reward of the Christian is more of what the Christian always wanted — the fellowship and service of the Lord Jesus Christ.

There is also a *human necessity.* This vile world is no friend of grace. Christians deserve a moment of vindication, celebration and elevation for the lives they have lived. Some ask why God would not have done that one-by-one as Christians go to be with Him? The answer is settled and simple. The influence of any Christian life continues long after that life is over.

For example, the sermons of Charles H. Spurgeon, who died in 1892, are still printed, read and preached all over the world. It is likely that on the day of the Rapture, someone somewhere will be blessed by a Spurgeon sermon. The reward of

Charles H. Spurgeon will come only after the full scope of his influence and blessing on others has been realized. In a lesser way that is true for all of us. The goodness, kindness and sanctity of a devoted Christian life has an influence far beyond itself. A grandmother influences a daughter who leads a granddaughter to Christ, and so it goes through the generations. There is a human necessity that we all appear before the Judgment Seat of Christ.

There is a *totality* of Christians that must appear before the Judgment Seat of Christ. *We must all appear...* We have all known people who miss appointments habitually. They may be charming, well-intentioned people, but they simply miss appointments. No Christian shall miss his or her appointment with the Judgment Seat of Christ.

Sometimes we think that the Judgment Seat of Christ will be for spectacular superstars of the Christian faith — Paul, Luther, Wesley or Graham. Others may think that the Judgment Seat of Christ is for those Christians who are saved "as by fire," a place of rebuke and warning for those saved but without reward. In fact, we shall all of us — every Christian of every age — appear before Christ at this judgment. The most common, ordinary, pedestrian Christian will be there. The deacon and the preacher, the usher and the youth leader, the singer and the pianist, the single mom and the aged missionary shall all of them have an individual time with the Lord Jesus Christ.

Think of it! You will stand before the Risen Lord Jesus Christ at His great *Bema,* His judgment seat. Most of us would be nervous to stand before the lowest court in our city, a mere small claims court. The thought of standing before a civil district court would give us distress. The idea of standing before the United States Supreme Court is beyond anything we can even imagine. Yet each believer has a destiny more daunting than that. We shall stand before Him Who loved us, died for us, rose for us and sits at the right hand of the Father for us.

There will be no empty chairs at God's great family court. At most homes someone may be missing from the table at Thanksgiving or at Christmas. There is an empty chair and an absence of someone who, through some necessity, is far away. There will be no such necessary absences at the Judgment Seat of Christ. We shall all be there.

Perhaps the most significant word about the Judgment Seat of Christ is *transparency*. There is the suggestion that we shall all be flooded with light at that moment. We shall be made manifest. We shall be raked over with that Light from which nothing shall be hidden. That Light will be like a heavenly MRI, seeing through us and revealing everything within us. For the Christian who loves the Lord Jesus Christ that is a *tremendous* moment, not a terrible moment. The desire of every born again believer is to be like Jesus. We wish to be like Jesus all day long, in the shop and in the home. Yet we fail. We fall short. The good that we would, we do not, and that which we would not, that we do. When we stand in the Light of the Judgment Seat, all of that which impeded and frustrated and retarded us will be burned away. We will be revealed to ourselves more than to Him. The Lord Jesus knows us, but we shall be made manifest to ourselves and in that moment "we shall see Him and be like Him, because we shall see Him as He is."

That great manifesting Light will also manifest us to others. There is a great deal of misunderstanding, limited compassion and harsh judgment even in the family of God. The brother next to us may have no idea what we are enduring. Some always think we should have done better, could have tried harder and might have achieved more. In that moment our true heart will be manifest. It will be shown who indeed loved the Lord. Others will see that we could have built pyramids for God, but we only had pebbles. We could have woven golden garments, but only had burlap thread. How much more some of us would have done if we only could have done it. In that great moment we shall be manifest in the truth of our motives, desires and longings to be and do and go for the Lord Jesus.

Unfortunately, that Light will also reveal as fool's gold what appeared to be true gold for the Kingdom of God. A complement to 2 Corinthians 4 is the great passage in 1 Corinthians 3:11-15. There Paul wrote of two ways to build on the foundation of the Lord Jesus Christ. Some Christians build with valuable materials: gold, silver and precious stones. Other Christians build with worthless materials: wood, hay and stubble. At the Judgment Seat of Christ the Light of a mighty fire will test the true value of every Christian life. Those who have built their Christian life with costly materials shall receive rewards. Those who have built their Christian life with worthless materials will be saved like a man running out of a burning building with nothing but the clothes on his back.

The background of this passage was the fire that would sometimes sweep through the Greek cities. The cities were a combination of beautiful marble temples and hovels made of straw. The fire would leave the great marble temples standing but would quickly consume the shanties made with the refuse of the street. Some Christians have built lives like temples; those lives shall stand the test of the fire because they were built with a lifetime of sacrificial service. Other Christians have lived more selfishly and built very little into their lives. They were saved, but that is all. Sacrifice, growth and abundant grace were strangers to them. They shall be saved through the fire with nothing but their salvation left. They will have no reward; they shall, in fact, "suffer loss." No one knows what that loss is, but the mere mention of it should chill the blood of every genuine Christian. Who wants to find out what that loss is?

Future Story
Helen Has Her Moment

Although Harold and Henry were nowhere near the Judgment Seat of Christ, Betty and Helen indeed awaited their appointment with the Master at His great Bema, or Judgment Seat. There was no long line with people floating around on clouds like the cartoons presented it. Actually, the worship of the Lamb on the Throne continued without ceasing. Betty, Helen and millions like them had been caught up to be with the Lord. Immediately and consciously they were in the presence of a great throng of worshippers around the Throne. One by one these appeared before the risen Lord Jesus Christ. There was no dread, only anticipation of seeing their Lord.

When Helen's time came, two joyous celestial beings greeted her as if she were an honored guest. They informed her that they had witnessed her entire life, and marveled at the redemptive power of God during her time on earth. In fact, they told her that they had actually studied the redemptive power of God in her life; the Lord had sent them to school watching Helen's growth as the primary demonstration of His great power. This caused a gasp of astonishment on the part of Helen.

Then, suddenly, she stood in the presence of the great Light. Radiating from the most caring face she had ever seen came a lustrous love. Mouth agape, eyes wide open, heart racing, she stood face to face with Jesus. Her mind went back to the times she sang the old gospel song, *Face to Face with Christ My Savior.* Here she was!

Then He called her by name, "Helen." Great warmth, like liquid love, suffused her entire being. She had never felt so much "at home" in all of her life. Safety, security, peace and unity flooded over her being.

Then He said, "Let us look at your life."

This began a review of her life from its first moment. There she was in her home, with her devout parents, going to Sunday school, visiting her grandmother and going to school. Yes, there were moments she was ashamed of and regretted having to view with Him. Yet every time one of those moments came, there was a rush of heat inside the light, like feeling the flash of a fire in the barbecue pit, and those moments disappeared. She watched the morning she professed her faith in Christ. She watched her baptism. She reviewed every moment of her life with Him. He smiled and often said to her, "Well done, good and faithful servant." It was just like the Bible said it would be.

Then the triumphant moment came. With His nail-scarred hands he picked up a crown, which looked like a beautiful laurel leaf with a golden hue, and placed it on her head. When He put it there, she felt more "alive" than she had ever felt. He told her, "Receive the crown of Life."

Then in an instant she was back again with the worshiping throng, singing praises to the Lamb on the Throne in the Light.

All Helen could say was, "Oh my!"

Chapter Seven

The World Gets What it Wants: Great Tribulation

Future Story

Daybreak in Normal, Ohio, witnessed an unparalleled scene. Henry Rhodes reached across the bed to feel the recumbent form of his saintly wife. Placing his hand on the sheets next to him, he felt an unfamiliar void. Henry *always* woke up first, *always* made the coffee and had done so every weekday and Saturday for the 25 years he had been married to Helen. The only exception was Sunday, when Helen quietly slipped out of bed to go to Normal Bible Church. Years ago they had come to a truce. Henry despised Christianity, preachers and the zany fundamentalists at Normal Bible Church. On the other hand, he adored Helen. She was totally faithful, always respectful and had the adornment of a meek and quiet spirit. He had often told himself that if all Christians were like her, he might be one.

Henry was the foreman at a tire plant. He thought he knew men, life and work. There was no place in his world for the spiritual or the thoughtful. The nearest thing to transcendence for Henry was the Sunday NFL game.

"Helen," he called out. He thought that Helen had gone out to the patio where sometimes they sat and admired their back yard. Or maybe she had gone out to get the paper. He decided to go outside to the front yard and see if she were there. As he stepped onto his porch, he noticed that Eva from down the street was talking to the teenage daughter of Stan and Marie next door. He went over to ask them if they had seen Helen.

Before he could say a word, Eva asked Henry if he had seen Jake, her husband. As he opened his mouth, Brandy — the daughter of Stan and Marie — asked the same thing about her parents. They were gone from their bedroom. There was no sign of the usual morning ablutions and preparations. In fact, the sheets of the bed were as if they had not been moved. Everyone stood quietly for a minute, awkward at such conversation but suddenly suspicious of something mysterious.

Then Oscar, the neighborhood grouch and troublemaker, ran out of his front door like he had been shot out of a gun. He wildly looked up and down the street. Spying the trio in conversation he screamed, "The *Today* show says that millions of people are missing this morning. On the interstates there are thousands of wrecks with no one in half the cars. A plane hit the World Trade Center on an approach to La Guardia and at least two dozen other planes have crashed."

The trio looked at him in blank astonishment.

The clueless Henry asked Oscar, "Have you seen Helen?"

Eva felt a cold shudder and the deepest fear she had ever felt. Her grandmother had taken her to church as a child. The old preacher used to talk about a day like this. People disappearing. Planes crashing. Car wrecks everywhere. Eva knew what had happened. She wretched right there on the street in front of her mailbox. Jake was a born-again Christian. She was a good woman, but never understood what he saw in all of that stuff down at the evangelical church. The trio watched her in astonishment.

"Jesus came back," she croaked out, as she grabbed her robe around her and let out a wail that scared everyone out of their wits.

Welcome to the first day of the Great Tribulation. The scene described above will not be fiction. It will one day be repeated all over the world. The world that despised Jesus, did not want His name mentioned in public prayer at the Rotary Club or the football game, ridiculed His followers on sitcoms and hated His church will get exactly what that world wants and deserves — a Christless, Churchless, Spiritless world.

We have already previewed what will happen to both the saved and the lost immediately at the time of death. We have even considered the wondrous Rapture of the Church and the judgment of Christians in heaven at the Judgment Seat of Christ. While these events take place in heaven, indescribable catastrophes will take place on the earth. We shall seek to describe in words what cannot be described. There is no doubt that the world will yet experience a time of "great tribulation."

The roadmap to that period may be found in

Revelation 6 through 19. These words were written by the aged apostle John on the tiny fist of rock called Patmos that juts out of the Aegean Sea, off the coast of Turkey. John was the last surviving eyewitness to Jesus among the original Twelve. The Romans imprisoned him on Patmos during the imperial reign of Domitian at the end of the first Christian century. Isolated, alone, separated from the churches he loved and wondering about the survival of Christianity in the face of the power of Rome, John suddenly experienced a revelation, the Revelation. The word is not plural — revelations — but singular. The book is one united and cohesive unveiling of the final victory of Christ over the might of Rome and every other empire that ever challenged the Lord Jesus Christ. As part of that vision, John saw those events which will transpire immediately after the Rapture.

Revelation belongs to a kind of writing that scholars call *apocalyptic*. This comes from the very meaning of the title of the book, Revelation. The word suggests the rending of a veil, the lifting of a curtain or the taking away of a shroud. Suddenly the great cosmic curtain was lifted and John saw what could be known only by a direct revelation from God. He saw the great drama of the final victory of Jesus Christ and His Church over all that resists it. A large part of that vision was the events of seven years after the Rapture. Those events are presented in picture language, in a dramatic code that seeks to present what words alone cannot describe. The great ballerina Petrovna was once asked what she meant by a certain dance. She responded, "If I could have said it, I would not have danced it." In a similar way, God showed John a series of pictures that said what words alone cannot say. These visions were inerrantly recorded in the Revelation.

At the center of the action is a scroll that is in the hand of the risen Christ. That scroll has been sealed seven times with sealing wax. The seals are broken open one at a time, and with the breaking of each seal another horrifying catastrophe envelopes the world without Christians and the Church. The seventh seal introduces the deafening peal of seven trumpets, the blowing of which heralds the coming of other catastrophes. The seventh trumpet inaugurates the pouring out of the wrath of God from seven bowls. Like the mighty caldrons in a steel factory shining with molten metal, the wrath of God will be poured out from bowls in heaven and its stinging, burning vengeance will scald the rebel planet that rejected His Son.

Reverent scholars do not all agree concerning the role of the Church in the Great Tribulation. There are those who believe in the so-called

Post-Tribulation Rapture. That is, the Church shall go through the tribulation along with the world. The Church on the earth shall experience all of the horrors of Revelation 6-19 during the outpouring of the wrath of God.

Still others have postulated the Mid-Tribulation Rapture. In that scenario, the church will go through the first three and one-half years of the Great Tribulation and then be rescued by the Rapture. Advocates of that view often rely upon certain interpretations of the prophecy of Daniel.

Our position is that the Church will be removed at the beginning of the Great Tribulation. Among other reasons supporting this, the Church disappears in the Revelation until it reappears at the end of Revelation 19. In Revelation 2 and 3 the Church is addressed by the risen Christ. In Revelation 4 the Apostle is invited to come up to heaven and to view the astonishing worship of the living creatures, the elders and the myriads around the throne of God. In Revelation 5 the crowned and reigning Christ is worshiped and considered worthy to open the book of human destiny, the scroll that contains the horrors and the punishments of the Great Tribulation.

Then there thunders from that exalted setting a cry from one of the intelligent creatures, one of the four living creatures, that summons John and all the rest of us, "Come and see." Those words must have rung in the ears of the aged apostle John. Some 60 years earlier on the first encounter with the Lord Jesus, the Master had told the first disciples who wished to know where he lived, *Come and see* (John 1:39). Now, after all the passing of the years, the risen, reigning, cosmic Christ sends another word. That word invites them to come and see the Great Tribulation.

Revelation Chapter Six

And I saw when the Lamb opened one of the seals, and I heard, as it were the noise of thunder, one of the four beasts saying, "Come and see." And I saw, and behold a white horse: and he that sat on him had a bow; and a crown was given unto him: and he went forth conquering, and to conquer.

And when he had opened the second seal, I heard the second beast say, "Come and see." And there went out another horse that was red: and power was given to him that sat thereon to take peace from the earth, and that they should kill one another: and there was given unto him a great sword.

And when he had opened the third seal, I heard the third beast say, "Come and see." And I beheld, and lo a black horse; and he that sat on him had a pair of balances in his hand. And I heard a voice in the midst of the four beasts say, "A measure of wheat for a penny, and three measures of barley for a penny; and see thou hurt not the oil and the wine."

And when he had opened the fourth seal, I heard the voice of the fourth beast say, "Come and see." And I looked, and behold a pale horse: and his name that sat on him was Death, and Hell followed with him. And power was given unto them over the fourth part of the earth, to kill with sword, and with hunger, and with death, and with the beasts of the earth.

And when he had opened the fifth seal, I saw under the altar the souls of them that were slain for the word of God, and for the testimony which they held: And they cried with a loud voice, saying, "How long, O Lord, holy and true, dost thou not judge and avenge our blood on them that dwell on the earth?" And white robes were given unto every one of them; and it was said unto them, that they should rest yet for a little season, until their fellow servants also and their brethren, that should be killed as they were, should be fulfilled.

And I beheld when he had opened the sixth seal, and, lo, there was a great earthquake; and the sun became black as sackcloth of hair, and the

*moon became as blood; And the stars of heaven
fell unto the earth, even as a fig tree casteth her
untimely figs, when she is shaken of a mighty
wind. And the heaven departed as a scroll when it
is rolled together; and every mountain and island
were moved out of their places.*

*And the kings of the earth, and the great men,
and the rich men, and the chief captains, and the
mighty men, and every bondman, and every free
man, hid themselves in the dens and in the rocks
of the mountains; And said to the mountains and
rocks, "Fall on us, and hide us from the face of
him that sitteth on the throne, and from the wrath
of the Lamb: "For the great day of his wrath is
come; and who shall be able to stand?" (King
James Version.)*

The Antichrist Comes

Surely one of the remarkable visions in the history of humanity is that of Revelation 6. The Lion/Lamb Christ opens one of the seals of the sealed scroll. Suddenly, on the stage of history, there appears a white horse and a warrior rider. From time immemorial a white horse has represented the conqueror's steed. From the ancients to the famous Traveler of General Robert E. Lee, a white horse resonates with the intent to wage war and to conquer. The Great Tribulation begins with the appearance of the Satanic masterpiece, the incarnation of all rapacious evil, the Antichrist. The Greek preposition *anti* has two meanings. It means (1) against, and (2) instead of. This evil human being will stand against everything Christ stands for and will take his place instead of the Lord Jesus, arrogating to himself those prerogatives and titles that should belong only to the Son of God. The world that would not have a real Christ will suffer the vengeance of an artificial Christ.

This figure should be identified with *the man of sin* in 2 Thessalonians 2:3,4. The appearance of this malevolent, diabolic mastermind will follow a great apostasy. There will be some decisive and marked falling away from the historic Christian faith just before the appearance of the Antichrist. This may typify the church before the Rapture or may involve merely professing Christians who cannot take the heat of persecution after the Rapture and who deny the faith. In the midst of this great falling away, this titanic, satanic figure will appear. He will sit in the rebuilt temple itself and receive the worship that belongs only to God.

Paul reminds the Thessalonians that this was part of the basic and rudimentary Christian teaching when he was with them (2 Thessalonians 2:5). Today, some critics condemn the teaching of Christian eschatology as scare tactics or idle speculation. Paul considered these matters a part of the kindergarten instruction given to the Thessalonians.

The Bible ransacks imagery to describe this final, evil manifestation. He is the first beast of Revelation 13, the little horn of Daniel 7:8, and the abomination of Matthew 24:15. In Revelation 13, a ferocious beast arises out of the stormy sea. In the Word the sea is always the symbol of the chaos and lawlessness of lost humanity.

Major Ian Thomas, a famous British evangelist, once told of seeing a picture on an office wall. Out of the raging sea there was a hand emerging. Each of the digits, instead of being a thumb or finger, was a human being. Each of the fingers was in a contorted, angry and hostile battle with the other fingers. Major Thomas considered it the epitome of lost humanity. Like fingers bound together on a hand, we are bound together. Yet we are grotesquely at war with one another.

Just like the striking image in the picture seen by the evangelist, even so the beast emerges out of the chaos of post-Rapture humanity. He will be the darling of CNN. He will dominate the headlines of the metropolitan dailies. *Time* will name him the man of the year. The United Nations will crown him the leader of humanity.

This figure will combine the charisma of all of

his predecessors who were symbols of the Antichrist to come. He will have the fierceness of a Genghis Khan, the wile of an Attila the Hun, the will of a Julius Caesar, the imperial arrogance of an Alexander the Great, the winsomeness of a Charlemagne, the splendor of a Louis XIV, the command of Napoleon and the evil intent of a Hitler. He will be the dreaded, terrible sum total of every one of his bloodthirsty precursors.

The prophecy of Daniel 9 records an incredible prediction of the career of this monstrous, hideous blasphemer. Daniel reports a period of 70 weeks of years, or 490 years from the decree of Artaxerxes to Nehemiah on March 14, 445 B.C. By exact calculation one finds that in the last of those "weeks," those septenary series of years, the Antichrist makes a covenant with Israel and sits in the temple itself in the form of his image. One can only imagine the catastrophic consequences of such a presence in the midst of the Israeli and Arab world. After three and one-half years, this disingenuous impostor will show himself for what he is and turn against the very people who enshrined him. The outworking of this is recorded in graphic detail in the Revelation.

The Horsemen of the Apocalypse

In the aftermath of the disclosure that this

Great Impostor will bring war and not peace, the fiery red horse appears (Revelation 6:4). He brings bloody war in his wake. The history of humanity is the history of waiting for the next war. Even after the "war to end all wars," the worst war in history took place. War will not stop. No political party or aggregation of nations or religious and humanitarian efforts will ever stop bloody war on a lost and rebellious planet. Yet the worst is yet to come. With the Church absent and with the Antichrist in charge, the world will be a river of blood.

In the wake of the fiery red horse will come the black horse of famine (Revelation 6:5). It will take a day's wages to buy a mere quart of wheat, a minute amount. Our food production and distribution system in the modern world is woefully thin. A global war will starve millions and millions. This planet will see powerful men wandering the streets of cities begging for the smallest amount of wheat to ward off starvation. The planet that rejected the Bread of Life will one day beg for bread.

Following the black horse is a pale horse, the spectral horse of Death itself. In the wake of war and famine, ghostly death will cover the planet like a horrible and polluted fog. One-fourth of humanity will die. If that were to happen in this generation, it would mean 250,000,000 corpses each in China and India. What an awful, ghastly, unimaginable carnage of lost humanity!

The thought of such plagues and disasters may seem far away, but it should not. Saddam Hussein has hidden away in secret biological laboratories deadly samples of anthrax. If a test tube of anthrax spores was released over New York City, much of the population would be obliterated. The same is true of the small pox virus also being hoarded by terrorists. There is only one dose of small pox vaccine for every 1,000 people in America. Terrible plague and awful death are distinct possibilities in a world with such malevolent intentions.

Future Story
Meanwhile Back with Henry Rhodes

When it finally dawned on Henry that the Rapture had taken place and that Helen was indeed caught away to be with the Lord, he spent some days in shock. He wandered around their empty house, half expecting Helen to come back. Then Henry became angry. How dare God take his sweet wife away in the Rapture! Henry had never liked the God Helen worshiped anyway. Now Henry was angry that God had taken her away. Then Henry became depressed. That was when he joined one of the thousands of

Rapture Support Groups that had sprung up around the country.

Meeting in a strip center near Henry's home, one of the government-supported Rapture Support Groups met on Monday nights. The federal government had given millions in grants to start such groups. With the massive disappearance of a significant portion of the nation's population, millions were depressed. Schools had lost their best teachers, hospitals their best nurses and businesses their best employees. Both Henry's supervisor and his best coworker were gone. On top of the stress of losing his wife to the Rapture, Henry had to work overtime to keep his beleaguered company from folding.

A member of the A.C.L.U., a secular humanist leader from the city's art community, led the Rapture Support Group. The group consisted of adults who had lost spouses or family members to the Rapture. They met on Mondays to discuss how they were feeling. Soon the group turned contentious, quarrelsome and confrontational. No one had a good answer for the obvious: Millions of people were gone and God seemed to have caused it. The group only depressed Henry and he dropped out after a month.

Strange as it may seem, after three months, Henry decided to go to church. Missing Helen terribly, afraid for his own destiny, he decided to go to the nearby Protestant church. The church had continued its regular round of weekly services without much change, other than the absence of approximately 40% of its congregation. The senior pastor, who had informed the members for years of the mythological background of the Bible, continued to stand in the pulpit each Sunday. He was not fazed by the disappearance of much of his congregation. He considered it in the larger context of history and existential existence and continued to give his bewildered congregation quotes from Sartre, Camus and *The New Yorker.* One by one the congregants decided he was more out of it than they were and had him fired by the board, most of whose members were still around to fire him.

Then when things looked the bleakest, events started to look more promising. Henry, who had always read *Time* and *Newsweek,* was entranced by the stories of a new leader rising from the populist movements in Eastern Europe. The man was welding together a huge coalition of people and appeared to have enormous charisma. Everything he said rang true and everything he did worked. Over the next few months Henry and millions with him were enthralled with the reports on CNN. This majestic man did nothing less than unite all of Europe under an emergency government formed because of the devastation of the Rapture.

In the months ahead, Henry watched the news and read the morning paper with a new obsession. The darling of Europe had flown to Washington and cemented a relationship with the President. Everything was looking promising, in fact, more promising that any time in Henry's life. Amidst all of the other remarkably progressive activities, the Jews in Jerusalem were rebuilding their ancient temple. *60 Minutes* and *20/20* devoted multiple programs to the striking rebuilding of the temple. It appeared as if there would be an unprecedented coalition of religion and politics, saving the planet from the disaster of the Rapture.

One Sunday morning as Henry was about to tune in to *Meet the Press*, a flash bulletin appeared beneath the NBC Peacock. The Great Leader was being welcomed into the new temple by the head rabbi of Jerusalem. The venerable Jewish leader suddenly appeared on the screen, along with the beaming presence of the Great Leader. To the shock of most of the planet, the Great Leader suddenly assumed the place in the temple that was supposed to be reserved for God Himself. The camera panned as a good number of the worshippers fell down before the Great Leader. Henry sat mesmerized in front of his television. It appeared that humanity would have a new beginning, all under the aegis of the Great Leader.

Suddenly, taking away his breath, Henry saw another news flash later in the morning. The Great Leader had turned from Dr. Jekyll to Mr. Hyde. As if out of nowhere, a massive army materialized and started a bloodbath. In the days to come, Henry watched as that bloodbath enveloped the Middle East, Europe, Africa and India. Terror struck the hearts of Americans as it appeared the marauding army would head for the riches of North America. Henry watched in horror as humanity's new darling turned into the great scourge of history. Henry was clueless that he was watching the career of the Antichrist.

The Wall Street Journal had been the first

to observe that the activities of the Antichrist (although no one called him that) were beginning to interrupt the food distribution channels. It came home to Henry when he went to the nearby Tom Thumb market and saw that the shelves held only one-half of their usual goods. Panic set in at the neighborhood. Once friendly neighbors jammed the aisles of the grocery stores and the teenage girls at the check out counters broke into tears as people literally grabbed food from one another's baskets. It was a chaotic scene out of some science fiction movie, Henry thought.

A month later, Henry sat in his leather recliner in total denial. He had just popped the last bag of popcorn. There was nothing else in the house to eat. The stores were empty and abandoned. The soup kitchens were overrun with people, but not their usual crowd. Brokers, attorneys, doctors and professors lined up, along with desperate street people, to eat some of the diminishing gruel that was passed out to the throngs. Henry had been there, but they ran out of food before he got to the window. So now he ate his last dish of popcorn.

And then Henry just sat there. Sirens

shrieked. The city's water and garbage system shut down because the workers were starving. The electricity went off two days later because no one had the strength to show up at the generating station. Henry just sat and looked at the wall. He put his hand on Helen's Bible and wished she were there to tell him everything would be all right.

Henry had just seen the beginning of the troubles. Soon he would understand.

Chapter Eight
The Last Great Battle

Future Story

Little did Henry Rhodes anticipate that as bad as things were, they would get much worse. As he scrounged the basement of his modest home for canned goods forgotten long ago, Henry sat by the hour watching what was left of CNN. With the failure of the power plants and the absence of the world's best technicians, the network only appeared now and then. Further, the power plant in Normal, Ohio, itself only produced power part of the time. Between the down time of the power plant and the off-the-air absences of CNN, Henry only caught sketches of world developments. For some of the developments, he only had to look out his front door.

The radical devotees of the Great Leader had developed a curious mark of their devotion, loathsome sores that cankered them and made them appear to be small pox victims. Those who lived near the coast reported that the sea had mysteriously turned a blood-red, and everything in it had died. The red-hued infestation of the ocean soon spread to the rivers and even the underground springs that fed them. The water supply of the world had turned to blood overnight. As if these miseries were not enough, global warming reached a new zenith. The unleashed power of the sun scorched man and beast with the greatest heat wave in world history. Henry sweltered in his recliner, warily watching the waning water in his five-gallon artesian water tank in the corner of the kitchen. The Everfresh water company had suddenly closed, only able to pump blood from its artesian source. Henry had no idea what he would do when that water was gone.

Nor had Henry seen anybody for weeks. One would have thought the adage "misery loves company" would have driven the lost souls in the neighborhood together. The Great Tribulation had exactly the opposite effect. People were so angry, depressed and suspicious of one another that they had barricaded themselves inside their homes. Except for occasional runs to the almost-empty store, no one dared to come outside for fear of being robbed and beaten by hungry neighbors. Henry slept more and more out of sheer depression.

Then Henry started to notice the escalating tensions in the Middle East. Always troubled and increasingly violent, the Middle East now dominated every newscast. Henry remembered the days when Arafat and Barak seemed to put the world on the edge of extinction. That was child's play compared to what was happening now. Infantry and armored divisions from the European commonwealth, masses of soldiers from China and a horde of armored divisions from the former USSR were headed toward a valley 15 miles from modern Haifa. The Great Leader and his counterpart, the Prophet, had fomented unrest in the earth that was leading toward the most senseless confrontation in history. In spite of all of the woes on the planet, the hordes of armies from every armed nation on the planet were converging on the Valley of Megiddo. Henry sat in a stupor as he watched the unfolding drama on the spasmodic availability of television. The blood lust of unredeemed human beings hurled the planet toward a great catastrophe.

Meanwhile in Heaven

Henry's wife Helen had never imagined such a "residence" could be hers, as if the mere human and temporal word *residence* even applied. After her session with the Lord Jesus Christ at His *Bema*, a wonderful time where she had gathered with her Christian family to celebrate the victories of faith in her temporal life, she had been rewarded with a lustrous white garment unlike anything she had ever seen. It constantly shone, but not with some garish Hollywood light. It shone with a gentle, warm light of purity and welcome. Two gigantic angelic beings had swept her along a golden path to a habitation. *Mansion* was not an adequate word. It was like a great mansion, but utterly different. Every window of it opened onto a view of the Light at the center, and the mighty worship that constantly took place there. The sweetest music imaginable swept through the windows that never had to be closed because the weather, if you could call it that, was more perfect than the best day she ever remembered in Normal, Ohio. Many considered the Ohio countryside to be beautiful, but nothing about it prepared Helen for the beauty she saw outside her windows. Even though she was alone and without Henry, she was not lonely. She still loved Henry, and knew that he was on earth in the Tribulation, but at the moment she had seen the risen Christ "she had known even as she was known," and was at peace with what had happened to poor Henry.

Then one day — if one could use the word since it was always *day* — there was a mighty and spontaneous movement toward the throne at the center of heaven. Millions and millions of triumphant believers gathered in endless concentric circles around the throne with a myriad of angels. Great praises rang out. The masses of saints from all the ages proclaimed, "Alleluia! For the Lord God Omnipotent reigns!" An electric sense of expectation thrilled the millions and millions. Something was about to happen.

A banquet hall was arranged for an event called, "The Marriage Supper of the Lamb." For hours, for days and days, the millions and millions celebrated the life and victories of the

Lord Jesus Christ. His eternal life as the Word of God before His incarnation at Bethlehem was celebrated. Then the entire multitude *saw* in review His entire earthly incarnation. It was not like a movie. It was just simply there, before them, presented by the God above all time. When he was born in the stable, the millions of the redeemed cried out "Hosanna!" All of them had loved and read their Bibles and had never imagined that they would be at a great banquet where His entire life — every episode of it — would be reviewed in a great setting of worship and praise. It defied all imagination.

A greater contrast between the despair that Henry felt and the elation that Helen felt could not be portrayed. As Henry ate his last can of ancient and stale spinach, Helen feasted at the Marriage Supper of the Lamb. No words could describe the difference in their circumstances.

At the penultimate moment of the Marriage Supper of the Lamb, a striking white horse appeared as if a Pegasus, but without wings. To the fanfare of a million trumpets the risen and ascended Lord Jesus Christ arose from beside the throne of Light, and with the angels as His equerries mounted the horse.

Fire flashed from His eyes. Multiple diadems were on His head. Then, as if under the command of an unseen General, a similar beautiful white horse appeared alongside each of the redeemed, including a startled Helen. In an instant, without effort, she was mounted on the white steed. The horse fell in with the millions of others in the perfectly timed cavalry of heaven. Helen laughed to herself and called it the "Calvary cavalry." At the head of this mighty army of mounted saints rode the Lord Jesus Christ. The golden streets of heaven thundered with the clopping of countless millions of hooves. Great "alleluias" ricocheted off the parapets of the heavenly city. Wonderment and awe filled each heart as the heavenly army rode behind the risen Lord Jesus Christ. The army was transported in an instant to the vicinity around Haifa. No one knew how, no one cared how and no one even wondered how. For now, every eye was fixed on the Son of God on the horse, awaiting His next command. Then it was over. There was no battle. The Great Leader, his Prophet, the bloodthirsty armies of the world — all of them simply surrendered. Not a shot was fired, not a bomb dropped, not a sword unsheathed, yet a river of blood flowed two hundred miles long and four and one-half feet deep. The Great Leader and the Prophet were hurled into the deep abyss of hell. Demons laughed. Birds of pray gorged on the dead. The Lion/Lamb had won the final battle without a shot being fired. Helen said to herself in her saintly Midwestern simplicity, "Oh, my!"

Henry Makes a Sudden Exit

Henry slept most of the time. The electricity was now gone. The heating oil people were long since out of business. There was nothing left to eat. The only water remaining was rainwater that Henry collected in a makeshift cistern. The house grew colder. The dog was skin and bones and had eaten nothing for a week. Without electricity Henry could not watch television, if there was any television to watch. The Internet was down, the radios were silent and the neighbors barricaded in their own houses. It finally began to dawn on depressed and denying Henry that he was going to die, and soon.

Indeed, Henry finally did die. The sum total of the deprivations of the Great Tribulation took their toll on Henry. In some mysterious way, he was further and further away from the life on earth he had known. A great Force propelled him through the universe toward a place of darkness and incredible heat. Even though he was not in a "bodily" existence, he nevertheless was experiencing consciousness, reality, heat and darkness. Finally, he had the ominous sense of being locked into something somewhere. It was totally dark, totally hot and absolutely miserable. The reality of his new home slowly dawned on Henry, he had died and gone to hell.

Chapter Nine

The Millennium and the Eternal Order

Revelation 20 –22

The risen Lord Jesus Christ will reign on a renewed earth in a kingdom that lasts for a thousand years. He gives us that assurance in His revelation. Satan, the deadly deceiver of the human race, will be chained in the bottom of his own hellish pit (Revelation 20:2). During that time the saints of the ages will rule with Him (Revelation 20:4). Think of it: We will reign with Christ!

There are three primary views of the millennial question. The amillennial view recognizes no reign of Christ on earth for a thousand years. In the Greek language, the letter "a" negates a noun and is the equivalent of saying "non-millennial" view. Advocates of this interpretation identify the reign of Christ with His reign in the church through the ages. They believe that all of Revelation until the passages on heaven at the very end, applied to the Roman Christians who first read the book. The non-millennialists further believe that there will be a general resurrection of believers and the lost, a general judgment and then the eternal order will begin. Dr. Ray Summers in his book *Worthy Is the Lamb* presents a fair understanding of this view.

The post-millennialists believe that the preaching of the gospel will so improve the world that a period of 1,000 years of righteousness will precede the return of the Lord Jesus Christ. The power of the gospel will transform the planet. Human society and life as we know it will be progressively sanctified until perfect peace breaks out.

In one way this gives great tribute to the power of the Gospel. In reality, however, this view is invalidated by the terrible events of the twentieth century. At the turn of that century it looked as if such a thing might happen. The violence of World War I all but killed such optimism and World War II certainly did. The cynicism of the '60s gave a deathblow to such hopes. A recognized advocate of this view was the founder of Southwestern Baptist Theological seminary, Dr. B. H. Carroll, in his commentary on Revelation, *Interpretation of the English Bible*.

I believe in the reign of the Lord Jesus Christ on earth for a thousand years. I am not alone. No one less respected than the great church historian Philip Schaff stated that.

> The most striking point in the eschatology of the ante-Nicene age [the period just after the New Testament was written] is the prominent chiliasm, or millenarianism, that is the belief of a visible reign of Christ in glory on earth with the risen saints for a thousand years, before the general resurrection and judgment. It was indeed not the doctrine of the church embodied in any creed or form of devotion, but a widely current opinion of distinguished teachers....[1]

We should understand some very significant landmarks in the development of the precious belief that our Lord Jesus Christ will reign in the world that rejected Him and nailed Him to the Cross. Even the Jews believed in a millennial reign of the Messiah during the period between the Old and New Testaments. In the Jewish devotional or apocalyptic writings there was the specific belief that the Messiah would reign for a thousand years.

Immediately following the writing of the New Testament, it was interpreted by a group of men collectively called the "church fathers." The Roman Catholic Church has claimed these men, but in reality they belong to all the Church. For the first 250 years of Christian history, there was no other view in writing other than the expectation that the Lord Jesus Christ would reign on the earth.

One of the earliest was Papias of Hierapolis, the bishop of the church in a small town in what is today Turkey. Irenaeus tells us that Papias had been personally related to "John the Elder," another name for the author of Revelation. In the principal work of Papias, which no longer exists but is referred to by other writers, Papias endorsed the view of the millennial reign of Christ. Now here is a man who personally knew the Apostle John and had the advantage of hearing John talk about the truths he wrote in the Revelation. I believe that Papias should certainly know more about what John meant in Revelation 20 than anyone alive today, and Papias believed in a millennial reign of Jesus Christ.

Justin Martyr (100/10-163/67) stands as one of the revered Greek Fathers of the Church. Justin was born in Samaria of pagan parents. He was converted to Christianity in Ephesus circa A.D. 130. He was beheaded for Jesus in Rome in A.D. 165. In his writings, Justin Martyr clearly championed the view of a reign by Jesus Christ on the earth from Jerusalem.

Irenaeus (120/40-202) stands out as a great

proponent of the reign of the Son on earth. He sat at the feet of Polycarp, an early martyr. He became bishop in Lyon, in what is today France, during the persecution of the church in A.D. 177. He strongly defended the reign of Christ on earth at the end of time. He is a particularly strong voice for the millennial reign of Christ because he was connected to the apostles through the voice of the famous martyr Polycarp.

Many others could be named, but it would become too technical. Hippolytus, an early bishop of Rome, advocated the reign of Christ. The very first commentary ever written on Revelation by Victorinus of Petau, part of modern Austria, advocated the reign of Christ on earth. Lactantius of North Africa believed in the millennial reign, as did Commodian of the same area. Methodius of Olympus also preached the reign of Christ. These heroes of the early church, some of whom lost their lives for what they believed and taught, are bright and shining lights advocating the reign of Jesus Christ on earth.

I mention these for you to understand that the reign of Christ is no modern invention by recent scholars. It was the only view the church knew for hundreds of years until later scholars began to deny it. I believe that Christ will reign on earth for a thousand years.

The Great Purging

When the last lost person has stood before the Great White Throne, there will be a fiery and noisy conflagration which will burn up both the heavens and the earth as we know them (2 Peter 3:10). This will be a firestorm of atomic proportions, which will consume everything in the heavens and on earth. After this purging fire, there will be "new heavens and a new earth in which righteousness dwells" (2 Peter 3:13). You should note carefully that Peter refers not only to a new heaven but also a new earth. He expected that this weary old earth will be purged in a mighty fire and will reappear in a new edition.

What God does is always incarnation, a downward movement. The Lord Jesus Christ came down from above to a stable in Bethlehem. In the same way, when John sees a new heaven and a new earth, the New Jerusalem comes *down* from above (Revelation 21:1-2). God will not preside over a new order that omits the earth from His plans. Rather, the Son of God will reign in power from the New Jerusalem. What a glorious day that will be when the reign of Jesus Christ covers the world! He will reign for a thousand years in glory and power with all of His saints.

Helen in the Millennium

While poor old Henry was in the darkness and the heat, Helen experienced a very different destiny. Following the defeat of the Great Leader, Helen, along with the countless millions of saints participated in the enthronement of the Lord Jesus Christ on His throne in Jerusalem. She was thrilled to see Peter, Andrew, James and John and the others as they sat in great thrones around Jesus. She remembered how different things had been in Jerusalem the final week of His earthly life and ministry. There was no Cross now, but rather a Crown. He no longer wore the clothes of a carpenter, but wore golden diadems of incredible beauty. From His throne, emissaries went out to the entire planet.

Helen wondered how things were in the renewed Ohio. She did not have long to wait. A mighty angel came to her mansion with a scroll in hand. The reigning Jesus was giving Helen an assignment to go back to the Cleveland/Akron area and to administer the kingdom of God in that area. Helen could not believe her eyes as she was suddenly whisked back to the area she had once known. It was the same, but then again, not the same. Lake Erie, once polluted and foul, now shone with a vivid aquamarine as if it were in the Caribbean. But the most incredible thing was downtown Cleveland. Its sooty buildings had all been replaced by similar buildings, but they were radiantly different. Helen remembered singing the old song, "Thine alabaster cities gleam, undimmed by human tears...." That had never been the case before, but now it was definitely the case. America was beautiful!

At the end of the thousand year reign of Christ, Helen returned, as if by the speed of light, to her beautiful mansion. There, she sat in comfort with the other saints while the awful events of the Great White Throne unfolded.

One by one, the lost of all the ages were brought before God. Harold and Henry also kneeled in the presence of God. First, the Book of Works was opened. Then, a voice from the throne uttered these words: "Harold, because you rejected the forgiving blood of Jesus, your works condemn you." Another book was opened. This was the "Book of Life of the Lamb." The final destiny for Harold was sealed when the Lord Jesus

Christ spoke these words: "Harold, I came to give you life, a life free from the power and wages of sin. Because you rejected that life, your name has been blotted out of the Book of Life. You will have no part in the new eternity that I have prepared for those who love and accept me." All Harold could do was bend his knee to worship Jesus Christ and confess that Jesus Christ is Lord. Following this confession, Harold, along with his son Henry and all the remaining unbelievers were cast into the lake of fire.

As the saints conversed with each other, they prepared for the great fire and noise that would come at the end of the events of the Great White Throne. Suddenly, the heavens themselves shook and roared and burned. All of the saints were untouched by this, with the exception that they seemed to shine more brightly when it was over.

Helen witnessed the coming events by some supernatural ability to see what was happening at all places, for she knew even as she was known.

She saw a new heaven and a new earth. She watched as the holy city, new Jerusalem, came down from God out of heaven. The beauty of this place was beyond imagination.

She wanted to cry, but no tears would come to her eyes. Finally, a voice rang out that filled the new eternal kingdom. *It is done. I am Alpha and Omega, the beginning and the end. I will give unto him that is athirst of the fountain of the water of life freely. He that overcometh shall inherit all things; and I will be his God, and he shall be my son.* This would be her eternal dwelling place.

[1] Philip Schaff, *History of the Christian Church,* vol. 2: *Ante-Nicene Christianity,* 6th ed. (New York: Charles Scribner's Sons, 1892), p. 854.

A FINAL WORD

There you have it. THE END! Most of the time when we go to the movies we know when it is about to end. However, life is not that way. Here one moment, gone the next! Hard to believe, but that's the way it is.

I personally settled the question of my eternal destiny when I was a mere six years old. My godly mother saw to it that I heard the truth of Jesus' saving grace and I gave my heart to Christ.

What about you? If I were to be called upon today to preach your funeral, could I speak of your love for God and your commitment to Jesus Christ and His Church? If not, why not do something about this right now? As long as you have breath it's not too late. Today, right now, is the time to give your life to the One who gave His for you, Jesus Christ. It's the right thing to do.

Accept Christ NOW, and one day we'll reign together with Him!